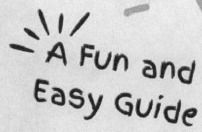
A Fun and Easy Guide

The Essential Young Chefs Cookbook

100+ SIMPLE AND DELICIOUS RECIPES FOR KIDS

LILLY WATSON

INTRODUCTION

Welcome to the wonderful world of cooking, where creativity meets the kitchen and every dish tells a story! The Essential Young Chefs Cookbook is your passport to a land of culinary adventures, designed especially for young chefs who are ready to explore the magic of cooking.

Whether you are cooking for the first time or looking to expand your skills, this cookbook offers over 100 recipes that will introduce you to the joys and simplicity of preparing food. From breakfasts that will have you jumping out of bed to snacks that are perfect for sharing with friends, each recipe is crafted with young cooks in mind, ensuring that the steps are straightforward and the outcomes are always delightful.

This book is not just about following recipes—it's about learning the ropes of the kitchen, understanding ingredients, and mastering basic cooking techniques that will serve you for a lifetime. You'll discover how to safely chop, mix, bake, and fry, transforming raw ingredients into dishes that will amaze your family and fill your home with joy.

But what makes cooking truly special? It's the fun you'll have every step of the way! Each page of this cookbook is packed with lively illustrations, fun facts, and tips that will spark your creativity and encourage you to experiment with flavors and textures. We've also included a guide on how to set your kitchen, choose the right tools, and even how to plate your dishes like a pro.

Whether it's a lazy Sunday afternoon, a festive birthday party, or a weeknight dinner with the family, The Essential Young Chefs Cookbook is your go-to resource for easy, tasty, and fun recipes. So tie on your apron, gather your ingredients, and get ready to cook, taste, and celebrate food with every meal you prepare!

Join us on this delicious journey and become the young chef you've always dreamed of being—happy cooking!

CONTENTS

Snack Attack **56**

Welcome to the Kitchen

UNDERSTANDING YOUR COOKING SPACE

Welcome to the heart of the home—the kitchen! This is where all the magic happens, from whipping up delicious meals to creating sweet treats. Before we dive into cooking, let's get to know our kitchen and learn how to stay safe while we have fun.

THE KITCHEN LAYOUT

The kitchen is like a playground, but instead of swings and slides, we have ovens, fridges, and countertops. Here's a quick tour of the most important spots:

The Refrigerator: This is where we keep things cold, like fruits, vegetables, milk, and juice. Remember to always close the door to keep the food fresh.

The Oven and Stove: This is where we cook and bake yummy meals. It's important to stay away from the stove when it's on and always use oven mitts when handling hot items.

The Sink: This is where we wash our hands and clean our dishes. Make sure to use soap and warm water to get rid of any germs.

The Countertops: These are the surfaces where we prepare our food. Keep them clean and organized so you have plenty of space to work.

KITCHEN SAFETY FIRST

Cooking is a lot of fun, but safety comes first! Here are some important rules to follow to make sure everyone stays safe in the kitchen:

Always Wash Your Hands: Before you start cooking, wash your hands with soap and water to keep your food clean.

Ask for Adult Help: If you're using sharp tools, the stove, or the oven, always ask an adult to help you. Never use these items without supervision.

Handle Hot Things Carefully: Use oven mitts when touching hot pans or dishes, and be careful around the stove.

Keep the Kitchen Clean: Clean up spills right away to avoid slips and keep your workspace tidy.

HYGIENE AND CLEANLINESS

A clean kitchen is a happy kitchen! Keeping things clean helps prevent germs from spreading and keeps your food safe to eat.

Wash Your Hands Often: Wash your hands before you start cooking, after touching raw ingredients, and after using the restroom.

Clean Your Workspace: Wipe down the countertops before and after cooking. Use a clean cloth or paper towel with warm, soapy water.

Wash Your Ingredients: Rinse fruits and vegetables under cold water before using them to remove dirt and bacteria.

Keep Raw and Cooked Foods Separate: Use different cutting boards for raw meats and vegetables to avoid cross-contamination.

Understanding your cooking space and following these simple rules will help you become a safe and confident chef in the kitchen. Remember, the kitchen is a place for creativity and fun, but it's important to always stay mindful of safety and cleanliness. Now that you know your way around, you're ready to start your culinary adventure!

Essential Kitchen Tools and Equipment

Before we start cooking, let's get to know some of the tools and equipment that will help us create delicious dishes. Think of these items as your cooking superheroes—they make everything easier and more fun! We'll also introduce some special tools designed just for young chefs like you.

BASIC TOOLS

These are the tools you'll use the most in the kitchen. They're simple, safe, and perfect for a variety of tasks.

- **Measuring Cups and Spoons:** These are used to measure ingredients like flour, sugar, milk, and spices. Make sure to use the right size for each recipe. Remember, using the correct amount of each ingredient is key to making a tasty dish.
- **Mixing Bowls:** You'll need a few different sizes of bowls for mixing ingredients. They can be made of plastic, glass, or metal. Choose the size that fits the job, like a big bowl for mixing batter and a small one for cracking eggs.
- **Spatulas:** A spatula is great for mixing and scraping. Use it to fold ingredients together or to spread frosting on a cake. Rubber spatulas are flexible and work well for scraping every bit of batter from a bowl.
- **Wooden Spoons:** Wooden spoons are sturdy and great for stirring hot foods on the stove. They don't conduct heat, so they stay cool to the touch.
- **Whisks:** A whisk is used to blend ingredients smoothly and add air to mixtures like eggs or batter. It's perfect for making fluffy scrambled eggs or a light and airy pancake batter.

COOKING APPLIANCES

These appliances help with cooking and baking, but remember, some of them can get very hot or require adult supervision.

- **Oven:** The oven is where we bake things like cookies, cakes, and casseroles. Always ask an adult for help when using the oven since it gets very hot.
- **Microwave:** A microwave is great for quickly heating up food. You can use it to melt butter, warm up leftovers, or make microwave mug cakes. Make sure to use microwave-safe containers and ask an adult to help if needed.
- **Stovetop:** The stovetop is used for cooking things in pots and pans, like boiling pasta or making soup. It's important to always have an adult around when using the stove.
- **Blender:** A blender is used for making smoothies, milkshakes, and purees. Make sure the lid is on tight before blending, and let an adult help you with this appliance.

SPECIAL TOOLS FOR YOUNG CHEFS

There are some tools made especially for kids that make cooking safe and fun.

- **Plastic Knives:** These are great for practicing your cutting skills. They're sharp enough to cut through soft fruits and vegetables but safe for kids to use with supervision.
- **Child-Friendly Cutting Boards:** These cutting boards are usually smaller and have non-slip grips to keep them in place. Use them to chop, slice, and dice ingredients.
- **Small Utensils:** Kid-sized utensils like mini whisks, spatulas, and rolling pins are easier to handle and perfect for little hands.

INGREDIENTS AND HOW TO MEASURE THEM

Understanding how to measure ingredients correctly is important in cooking. Here's how to get it right:

- **Dry Ingredients:** Use measuring cups for dry ingredients like flour, sugar, and oats. Scoop the ingredient into the cup and level it off with a flat edge, like the back of a knife, to make sure you have the right amount.
- **Liquid Ingredients:** Use a liquid measuring cup for ingredients like milk, oil, or water. Place the cup on a flat surface and pour the liquid in. Check the measurement at eye level to be accurate.
- **Measuring Spoons:** Use these for small amounts of ingredients like salt, baking powder, or vanilla extract. Scoop or pour the ingredient into the spoon and level it off for the right amount.

READING RECIPES

Every great chef follows a recipe, especially when they're just starting out. Here's how to read a recipe so you know what to do:

- **Ingredients List:** This is where you'll find all the items you need to make the dish. Gather everything before you start cooking.
- **Step-by-Step Instructions:** Recipes are usually broken down into simple steps. Read through all the steps before you begin, so you know what to expect.
- **Prep and Cook Time:** This tells you how long it will take to prepare and cook the dish. Make sure you have enough time to finish before you start.
- **Servings:** This shows how many people the recipe will serve. It helps you know if you need to make more or less.

Now that you're familiar with your kitchen tools and how to use them, you're one step closer to becoming a master chef! Having the right tools and knowing how to use them makes cooking easier and more fun. Remember, always ask for help when you need it and enjoy the process of creating something delicious!

11

Cooking Skills for Young Chefs

Basic Cutting Techniques and Knife Safety

Now that you've got a handle on the kitchen tools and equipment, it's time to learn some cooking skills that every young chef needs to know. One of the most important skills is learning how to safely and properly cut ingredients. Remember, cooking involves using knives and other sharp tools, so safety is our top priority. Let's dive into some basic cutting techniques and safety tips that will help you become a confident and safe chef in the kitchen.

KNIFE SAFETY RULES

Knives are essential tools in the kitchen, but they need to be used with care. Here are some important rules to follow when handling knives:

Always Ask for Adult Supervision: Before using a knife, make sure an adult is nearby to supervise and help if needed. Never use sharp tools without permission and supervision.

Use the Right Knife: Start with a child-safe or plastic knife, which is designed to be safe for kids. These knives are sharp enough to cut soft fruits and vegetables but are safer than regular kitchen knives.

Keep Fingers Away from the Blade: When cutting, always hold the food with your fingers curled under, like a claw. This way, your fingertips are tucked away from the blade.

Cut on a Stable Surface: Always use a cutting board to protect the countertops and to give you a stable surface to work on. Make sure the cutting board is placed on a flat, non-slip surface.

Walk with the Knife Pointing Down: If you need to move with a knife, hold it securely by the handle with the blade pointing down towards the floor. This helps prevent accidents if you bump into someone.

BASIC CUTS

Learning some basic cutting techniques will make preparing food easier and more fun. Let's go over a few simple cuts that you can practice with an adult's help.

- **Slicing:** Slicing is used to cut food into thin, flat pieces. For example, you might slice cucumbers, strawberries, or bell peppers. To slice safely, place the food on the cutting board and use a rocking motion with the knife, keeping your fingers in a claw shape to hold the food steady.
- **Dicing:** Dicing means cutting food into small, even cubes. You can dice ingredients like carrots, apples, or cheese. First, slice the food into thin strips, then turn those strips and cut them into small cubes. Remember to keep your fingers curled and out of the way.
- **Chopping:** Chopping is a quicker way to cut food into pieces that don't need to be perfect or even. It's great for herbs like parsley or cilantro, as well as vegetables like onions. Use a gentle, up-and-down motion with the knife, and remember to hold the food securely with your claw hand.
- **Mincing:** Mincing is used to cut food into very small, fine pieces. This technique is often used for garlic, ginger, or herbs. Start by finely chopping the food, then run the knife back and forth over the pieces until they are very small.

USING OTHER CUTTING TOOLS

Knives aren't the only tools you'll use for cutting in the kitchen. There are other handy tools that make chopping, slicing, and grating easier and safer.

- **Peelers:** A peeler is used to remove the skin from fruits and vegetables, like potatoes, carrots, and apples. Hold the food firmly with one hand and the peeler with the other. Always peel away from your body to avoid any accidents.
- **Graters:** Graters are used to shred foods like cheese, carrots, and zucchini. They have small holes that cut the food into fine pieces. Hold the grater steady with one hand and slide the food up and down with the other. Be careful with your fingers near the grater—use the flat palm of your hand to push the food against the grater.
- **Kitchen Scissors:** Kitchen scissors are great for snipping herbs, cutting pizza slices, or trimming dough. They're easier to use than knives for some tasks and can be safer for little hands.

PRACTICE AND PATIENCE

Just like learning to ride a bike, using knives and other cutting tools takes practice. Start with softer foods like bananas or cucumbers and work your way up to harder ingredients as you become more comfortable. Remember, there's no rush—take your time, focus on safety, and have fun with it!

Learning to cut safely is an important step in becoming a skilled chef. By practicing these basic techniques and following safety rules, you'll be well on your way to chopping, slicing, and dicing like a pro. Just remember, the more you practice, the better you'll get. So grab your child-safe knife, get an adult to help, and start practicing your new cutting skills. Happy chopping!

Mixing, Stirring, and Folding

Great job mastering the basics of cutting! Now it's time to explore another essential set of skills that every young chef needs: mixing, stirring, and folding. These techniques help combine ingredients to make delicious dishes, whether you're whipping up a fluffy cake batter or a smooth pancake mix. Let's dive into these fun and fundamental cooking skills!

MIXING

Mixing is one of the most common tasks in cooking and baking. It's simply the process of combining ingredients until they're evenly distributed. There are different ways to mix, depending on what you're making:

Whisking: This is a fast way to mix ingredients to make them smooth and add air, which makes them light and fluffy. You'll use a whisk for tasks like beating eggs, mixing pancake batter, or whipping cream. Hold the whisk with one hand and the bowl with the other, and move the whisk in a circular motion to blend everything together.

Using a Spoon or Spatula: For thicker mixtures like cookie dough or mashed potatoes, a spoon or spatula is your best friend. You'll use a back-and-forth or circular motion to mix the ingredients. When using a spatula, it's great for scraping the sides of the bowl to make sure everything gets mixed in.

Electric Mixer: An electric mixer can make mixing easier, especially for things like cake batter or frosting. It has beaters that spin quickly to blend ingredients together. Always start on a low speed to avoid splattering, and make sure an adult is nearby to help if you're using an electric mixer.

STIRRING

Stirring is a gentle way of mixing ingredients together, often while cooking on the stove. It helps combine ingredients evenly and prevents them from sticking to the pan or burning:

Stirring on the Stovetop: When cooking things like soup, sauce, or scrambled eggs, you'll often stir with a wooden spoon. Use a

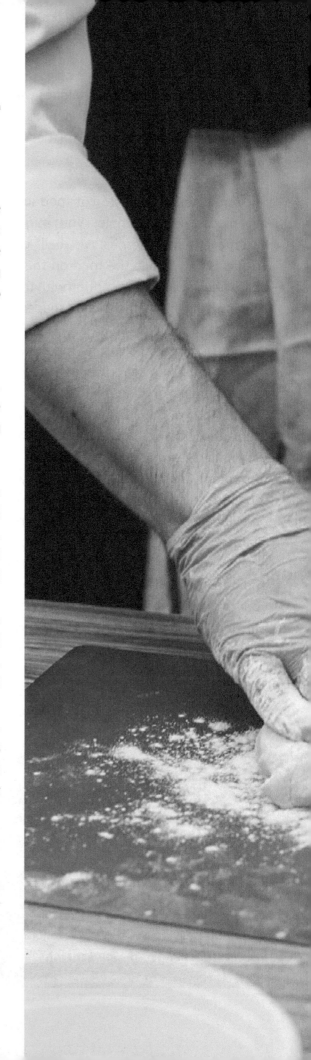

gentle circular motion, moving the spoon around the pan to keep everything cooking evenly.

Stirring Cold Ingredients: Stirring isn't just for hot foods! You'll also stir ingredients when making things like fruit salad or mixing a bowl of yogurt with granola. It's an easy way to combine ingredients without adding air or changing the texture.

Preventing Sticking: When stirring on the stovetop, it's important to keep the food moving, especially if you're cooking something thick like oatmeal or a creamy sauce. This prevents the food from sticking to the pan and burning.

FOLDING

Folding is a special technique used to gently combine ingredients without losing any of the air that's been added. It's often used in baking when you need to mix something delicate, like whipped egg whites or whipped cream, into a batter:

How to Fold: To fold ingredients, use a rubber spatula. Scoop under the mixture and fold it over the top. Turn the bowl slightly with each fold and continue until the ingredients are just combined. The goal is to keep the mixture light and airy, so be gentle and take your time.

When to Fold: You'll use folding when making things like meringue, soufflé, or fluffy cakes. It's also used when combining a delicate mixture, like whipped cream, into a thicker batter.

Practice Makes Perfect: Folding can be a bit tricky at first, but with a little practice, you'll get the hang of it. Remember to be gentle and avoid stirring too vigorously to keep the mixture light and fluffy.

BLENDING AND PUREEING

Sometimes, you'll need to blend ingredients into a smooth mixture or puree fruits and vegetables. Here's how to do it safely:

Using a Blender: Blenders are great for making smoothies, soups, and sauces. Just place the ingredients in the blender, secure the lid, and blend until smooth. Always make sure the lid is on tight, and start with a low speed to avoid splatters. If the mixture is thick, use the pulse button to blend in short bursts.

Handheld Blender: A handheld blender, also known as an immersion blender, can be used directly in the pot or bowl. It's perfect for pureeing soups or sauces. Make sure the blade is fully submerged in the food before turning it on, and keep your fingers away from the blade.

15

Rise and Shine
Breakfasts

Berry Fun Yogurt Parfait

2
SERVINGS

10 MINS
PERP TIME

00 MINS
COOK TIME

INGREDIENTS

1 cup plain Greek yogurt
1 cup mixed berries
(strawberries, blueberries,
raspberries)
1/4 cup granola
2 tablespoons honey
(optional)
2 tablespoons chopped
almonds (optional)

INSTRUCTIONS

1. In two small bowls or glasses, add ¼ cup of yogurt to the bottom
   of each. Layer mixed berries on top of the yogurt.
2. Sprinkle one tbsp granola over the berries in each bowl. Repeat
   the layers with the leftover yogurt, berries, and granola.
3. Drizzle honey and spread chopped almonds if desired.

NUTRITIONAL VALUES (PER SERVING):

Calories: 220, Protein: 11g,
Carbohydrates: 34g, Fat: 7g, Fiber: 5g

Scrambled Egg Muffins

INGREDIENTS

6 large eggs
1/4 cup milk
1/2 cup shredded cheddar cheese
1/2 cup diced bell peppers
1/4 cup diced ham (optional)
Salt and pepper to taste

4
SERVINGS

10 MINS
PERP TIME

20 MINS
COOK TIME

INSTRUCTIONS

1. Preheat oven to 350°F (180°C). Grease a muffin tin.
2. In a deep-bottom bowl, toss the eggs and milk until smooth.
3. Stir in the shredded cheese, bell peppers, ham (if using), salt, and pepper.
4. Ladle egg mixture into the muffin tin, filling each cup about 3/4 full.
5. Bake for 20 minutes or until the muffins are firm and slightly golden. Let cool before serving.

NUTRITIONAL VALUES (PER SERVING):

Calories: 180, Protein: 13g,
Carbohydrates: 3g, Fat: 12g, Fiber: 0g

Easy Peasy French Toast Sticks

INGREDIENTS

4 slices of bread
2 large eggs
1/4 cup milk
1/2 teaspoon cinnamon
1 teaspoon vanilla extract
1 tablespoon butter
Maple syrup for serving
(optional)

2	**5 MINS**	**10 MINS**
SERVINGS	PERP TIME	COOK TIME

INSTRUCTIONS

1. Cut each slice of bread into three strips to make sticks.
2. In a deep-bottom bowl, toss eggs, milk, cinnamon, and vanilla.
3. Heat butter in a pan.
4. Dip each breadstick into the egg mixture, making sure it's fully coated.
5. Cook on one side in the pan for 2-3 minutes until golden brown. Serve with maple syrup, if desired.

NUTRITIONAL VALUES (PER SERVING):

Calories: 250, Protein: 10g,
Carbohydrates: 30g, Fat: 10g, Fiber: 2g

19

Apple Cinnamon Oatmeal Cups

INGREDIENTS

1 1/2 cups rolled oats
1/2 teaspoon cinnamon
1 teaspoon baking powder
1/4 teaspoon salt
1 cup milk
1/4 cup honey
1 large apple, diced
1 large egg, beaten

4
SERVINGS

10 MINS
PERP TIME

25 MINS
COOK TIME

INSTRUCTIONS

1. Preheat oven to 350°F (180°C). Grease a muffin tin.
2. In a deep-bottom bowl, mix the oats, cinnamon, baking powder, and salt.
3. Stir in the milk, honey, diced apple, and beaten egg.
4. Drop the mixture into the muffin tin, filling each cup about 3/4 full.
5. Bake for 25 minutes until the cups are set. Let cool before serving.

NUTRITIONAL VALUES (PER SERVING):

Calories: 210, Protein: 6g,
Carbohydrates: 36g, Fat: 4g, Fiber: 4g

Cheesy Breakfast Quesadilla

1
SERVINGS

5 MINS
PERP TIME

5 MINS
COOK TIME

INGREDIENTS

1 large flour tortilla
1/2 cup shredded cheddar
cheese
1 large egg
1 tablespoon butter
Salt and pepper to taste

INSTRUCTIONS

1. In a small pan, scramble the egg with salt and pepper, then set aside.
2. Heat butter in a pan and place the tortilla in the pan.
3. Sprinkle half of the cheese on one side of the tortilla, add the scrambled egg, and top with the remaining cheese.
4. Fold the tortilla and cook
5. the other sides. Slice into wedges and serve warm.

NUTRITIONAL VALUES (PER SERVING):

Calories: 350, Protein: 15g,
Carbohydrates: 30g, Fat: 20g, Fiber: 2g

Chocolate Chip Mini Muffins

INGREDIENTS

1 cup all-purpose flour
1/2 teaspoon baking powder
1/4 teaspoon baking soda
1/4 cup sugar
1/4 cup melted butter
1 large egg
1/2 cup milk
1/4 cup mini chocolate chips

12 muffins
SERVINGS

10 MINS
PERP TIME

12 MINS
COOK TIME

INSTRUCTIONS

1. Preheat oven to 350°F (180°C). Grease a mini muffin tin.
2. In a deep-bottom bowl, mix the flour, baking powder, baking soda, and sugar.
3. In another deep-bottom bowl, toss the melted butter, egg, and milk.
4. Pour the wet elements into the dry ingredients and stir until just combined.
5. Fold in the mini chocolate chips. Fill the muffin tin about 2/3 full.
6. Bake for 12 minutes until a tooth-stick is inserted and comes out clean. Let cool before serving.

NUTRITIONAL VALUES (PER SERVING):

Calories: 110, Protein: 2g,
Carbohydrates: 15g, Fat: 5g, Fiber: 0g

Rainbow Fruit Salad with Honey Drizzle

INGREDIENTS

1 cup strawberries, sliced
1 cup blueberries
1 cup kiwi, diced
1 cup pineapple chunks
1 cup red grapes, halved
2 tablespoons honey
1 tablespoon lemon juice

4
SERVINGS

10 MINS
PERP TIME

00 MINS
COOK TIME

INSTRUCTIONS

1. In a deep-bottom bowl, combine all the fruit.
2. In a small, deep-bottom bowl, mix the honey and lemon juice.
3. Drizzle honey mixture over the fruit and gently toss to coat.
4. Serve immediately.

NUTRITIONAL VALUES (PER SERVING):

Calories: 120, Protein: 1g,
Carbohydrates: 31g, Fat: 0g, Fiber: 5g

Peanut Butter and Banana Toast

INGREDIENTS

1 slice whole grain bread, toasted
2 tablespoons peanut butter
1 small banana, sliced

1
SERVINGS

5 MINS
PERP TIME

00 MINS
COOK TIME

INSTRUCTIONS

1. Toast the slice of bread. Spread peanut butter evenly over the toast.
2. Arrange the banana slices on top of the peanut butter. Serve immediately.

NUTRITIONAL VALUES (PER SERVING):

Calories: 250, Protein: 7g,
Carbohydrates: 33g, Fat: 11g, Fiber: 5g

Blueberry Overnight Oats

1
SERVINGS

5 MINS
PERP TIME

00 MINS
COOK TIME

INGREDIENTS

1/2 cup rolled oats
1/2 cup milk (or almond milk)
1/4 cup Greek yogurt
1/4 cup fresh blueberries
1 tablespoon honey
1/4 teaspoon vanilla extract

INSTRUCTIONS

1. In a wide-mouth jar or container, combine oats, milk, yogurt, honey, and vanilla extract.
2. Stir in the blueberries. Cover and refrigerate overnight.
3. In the morning, stir and enjoy, adding more blueberries if desired.

NUTRITIONAL VALUES (PER SERVING):

Calories: 250, Protein: 10g,
Carbohydrates: 40g, Fat: 5g, Fiber: 5g

Veggie and Cheese Omelet

INGREDIENTS

2 large eggs
2 tablespoons milk
1/4 cup diced bell peppers
1/4 cup shredded cheddar cheese
Salt and pepper to taste
1 tablespoon butter

1
SERVINGS

5 MINS
PERP TIME

5 MINS
COOK TIME

INSTRUCTIONS

1. In a deep-bottom bowl, toss the eggs, milk, salt, and pepper.
2. Heat butter in a small pan and sauté the diced bell peppers until soft.
3. Drop the egg mixture into the pan and cook until the edges begin to set.
4. Sprinkle the cheese over one side of the omelet and fold it in half.
5. Cook more for 1-2 minutes until the cheese is melted. Serve warm.

NUTRITIONAL VALUES (PER SERVING):

Calories: 260, Protein: 16g,
Carbohydrates: 4g, Fat: 20g, Fiber: 1g

Cinnamon Roll Bites

INGREDIENTS

1 tube refrigerated crescent roll dough
2 tablespoons butter, melted
2 tablespoons sugar
1 teaspoon cinnamon
1/4 cup powdered sugar
1 tablespoon milk (for glaze)

4
SERVINGS

10 MINS
PERP TIME

12 MINS
COOK TIME

INSTRUCTIONS

1. Preheat oven to 350°F (180°C). Grease a baking sheet.
2. Roll out the crescent dough and cut it into small bite-sized pieces.
3. Mix the cinnamon and sugar in a small, deep-bottom bowl. Dip each dough bite in melted butter, then roll in the cinnamon-sugar mixture.
4. Place the bites on the baking sheet and bake for 10-12 minutes or until golden brown.
5. In a small, deep-bottom bowl, mix powdered sugar and milk to make the glaze. Drizzle over the cinnamon bites and serve warm.

NUTRITIONAL VALUES (PER SERVING):

Calories: 210, Protein: 2g,
Carbohydrates: 26g, Fat: 11g, Fiber: 0g

BREAKFAST BAGEL PIZZA

INGREDIENTS

1 whole wheat bagel, halved
1/4 cup pizza sauce
1/4 cup shredded mozzarella
cheese
2 slices turkey bacon, cooked
and crumbled
1 tablespoon diced bell
peppers (optional)

1
SERVINGS

5 MINS
PERP TIME

10 MINS
COOK TIME

INSTRUCTIONS

1. Preheat oven to 400°F (200°C).
2. Spread pizza sauce on each bagel piece.
3. Sprinkle mozzarella cheese on top, followed by turkey bacon and bell peppers if using.
4. Place the bagel halves on the paper-arranged baking sheet. Bake for 8-10 minutes until the cheese turns bubbly. Serve warm.

NUTRITIONAL VALUES (PER SERVING):

Calories: 300, Protein: 16g,
Carbohydrates: 38g, Fat: 10g, Fiber: 4g

Mini Breakfast Burritos

2
SERVINGS

10 MINS
PERP TIME

15 MINS
COOK TIME

INGREDIENTS

4 small flour tortillas
4 large eggs
1/4 cup shredded cheddar cheese
1/4 cup diced tomatoes
1/4 cup diced bell peppers
Salt and pepper to taste
1 tablespoon butter

INSTRUCTIONS

1. In a small pan, melt butter over medium heat. Scramble the eggs, adding salt and crushed pepper to taste.
2. Warm the tortillas.
3. Divide scrambled eggs evenly among the tortillas. Top each with cheese, diced tomatoes, and bell peppers.
4. Roll the tortillas into mini burritos and serve immediately.

NUTRITIONAL VALUES (PER SERVING):

Calories: 320, Protein: 18g,
Carbohydrates: 25g, Fat: 17g, Fiber: 2g

FUNFETTI WAFFLES WITH SPRINKLES

2
SERVINGS

5 MINS
PERP TIME

5 MINS
COOK TIME

INGREDIENTS

1 cup waffle mix
3/4 cup milk
1 tablespoon melted butter
1 teaspoon vanilla extract
2 tablespoons rainbow sprinkles
Maple syrup for serving (optional)

INSTRUCTIONS

1. Preheat the waffle iron.
2. In a deep-bottom bowl, mix the waffle mix, milk, melted butter, and vanilla extract.
3. Stir in the rainbow sprinkles.
4. Pour the batter into the waffle iron. Cook according to the steps mentioned on the manufacturer's guidelines until golden brown.
5. Serve with maple syrup if desired.

NUTRITIONAL VALUES (PER SERVING):

Calories: 290, Protein: 6g,
Carbohydrates: 43g, Fat: 10g, Fiber: 1g

Avocado Toast with a Sunny Side-Up Egg

INGREDIENTS

1 slice whole grain bread, toasted
1/2 avocado, mashed
1 large egg
Salt and pepper to taste
1 teaspoon olive oil

1
SERVINGS

5 MINS
PERP TIME

5 MINS
COOK TIME

INSTRUCTIONS

1. In a small pan, heat one tsp oil and cook the egg on the sunny side until the whites are set but the yolk is still runny.
2. Spread mashed avocado on the toasted bread and sprinkle with salt and pepper.
3. Place the sunny-side-up egg on top of the avocado toast and serve immediately.

NUTRITIONAL VALUES (PER SERVING):

Calories: 290, Protein: 10g,
Carbohydrates: 20g, Fat: 21g, Fiber: 6g

Breakfast Banana Splits

INGREDIENTS

1 banana, peeled and sliced
1/2 cup Greek yogurt
1/4 cup granola
1/4 cup mixed berries
(strawberries, blueberries,
raspberries)
1 tablespoon honey (optional)

1
SERVINGS

5 MINS
PERP TIME

00 MINS
COOK TIME

INSTRUCTIONS

1. Place the banana halves in a shallow bowl or plate.
2. Spoon the Greek yogurt over the middle of the banana slices.
3. Top with granola and mixed berries.
4. Drizzle with honey if desired, and enjoy!

NUTRITIONAL VALUES (PER SERVING):

Calories: 300, Protein: 10g,
Carbohydrates: 55g, Fat: 6g, Fiber: 7g

Sweet Potato Breakfast Hash

INGREDIENTS

1 large sweet potato, peeled and diced
1/2 small onion, diced
1/2 bell pepper, diced
2 large eggs
1 tablespoon olive oil
Salt and pepper to taste
1/4 cup shredded cheddar cheese (optional)

2
SERVINGS

10 MINS
PERP TIME

20 MINS
COOK TIME

INSTRUCTIONS

1. Heat one tbsp oil in a pan. Add diced sweet potato, onion, and bell pepper.
2. Cook for 10-15 minutes.
3. Push the veggies to one side and drop the cracked eggs on the empty side. Cook until the eggs are set.
4. Sprinkle cheese on top, and serve immediately.

NUTRITIONAL VALUES (PER SERVING):

Calories: 260, Protein: 10g,
Carbohydrates: 30g, Fat: 12g, Fiber: 5g

Nutella and Strawberry Breakfast Wraps

INGREDIENTS

1 small flour tortilla
2 tablespoons Nutella
4 strawberries, sliced
1 tablespoon chopped
almonds (optional)

1
SERVINGS

5 MINS
PERP TIME

00 MINS
COOK TIME

INSTRUCTIONS

1. Spread Nutella evenly over the tortilla.
2. Arrange the strawberry slices on top.
3. Sprinkle with chopped almonds if desired, then roll up the tortilla and enjoy.

NUTRITIONAL VALUES (PER SERVING):

Calories: 300, Protein: 6g,
Carbohydrates: 40g, Fat: 15g, Fiber: 3g

Rainbow Smoothie Parfaits

INGREDIENTS

1/2 cup strawberries
1/2 cup mango chunks
1/2 cup spinach
1/2 cup blueberries
1 cup Greek yogurt
1/4 cup granola

2
SERVINGS

10 MINS
PERP TIME

00 MINS
COOK TIME

INSTRUCTIONS

1. Blend the strawberries with a little water to create a smooth layer. Pour into two serving glasses.
2. Repeat with the mango, spinach, and blueberries, creating separate layers for each fruit.
3. Top with Greek yogurt and granola. Serve immediately.

NUTRITIONAL VALUES (PER SERVING):

Calories: 250, Protein: 10g,
Carbohydrates: 38g, Fat: 6g, Fiber: 5g

Lunchtime Fun

Rainbow Veggie Wraps

2
SERVINGS

10 MINS
PERP TIME

00 MINS
COOK TIME

INGREDIENTS

2 large whole wheat tortillas
1/4 cup hummus
1/4 cup shredded carrots
1/4 cup sliced bell peppers
1/4 cup cucumber, sliced into thin strips
1/4 cup spinach leaves
1/4 cup cherry tomatoes, halved

INSTRUCTIONS

1. Spread two tbsp hummus evenly over each tortilla.
2. Layer the carrots, bell peppers, cucumber, spinach, and cherry tomatoes on each tortilla, creating a colorful "rainbow" of veggies.
3. Roll up the tortillas tightly and secure them in half. Serve immediately.

NUTRITIONAL VALUES (PER SERVING):

Calories: 250, Protein: 8g,
Carbohydrates: 38g, Fat: 8g, Fiber: 8g

MINI MARGHERITA PIZZAS

INGREDIENTS

2 English muffins, halved
1/4 cup pizza sauce
1/2 cup shredded mozzarella cheese
4 fresh basil leaves
1 small tomato, sliced

2
SERVINGS

5 MINS
PERP TIME

10 MINS
COOK TIME

INSTRUCTIONS

1. Preheat oven to 400°F (200°C).
2. Spread pizza sauce over each half of the English muffin.
3. Top with shredded mozzarella cheese, a slice of tomato, and a basil leaf.
4. Place the mini pizzas on the baking sheet and bake for 8-10 minutes. Serve warm.

NUTRITIONAL VALUES (PER SERVING):

Calories: 280, Protein: 14g,
Carbohydrates: 34g, Fat: 10g, Fiber: 3g

Cheesy Quesadilla Pockets

INGREDIENTS

2 small flour tortillas
1/2 cup shredded cheddar
cheese
1/4 cup black beans (optional)
1 tablespoon butter

2
SERVINGS

5 MINS
PERP TIME

5 MINS
COOK TIME

INSTRUCTIONS

1. Put the pan over medium heat to melt the butter.
2. Place one tortilla in the pan and sprinkle with cheddar cheese and black beans if using.
3. Fold the tortilla in half to form a pocket and cook for 2-3 minutes on one side or until the cheese is melted and the tortilla is golden brown.
4. Remove from the pan, slice in half, and serve warm.

NUTRITIONAL VALUES (PER SERVING):

Calories: 270, Protein: 10g,
Carbohydrates: 28g, Fat: 13g, Fiber: 3g

Turkey and Cheese Roll-Ups

INGREDIENTS

4 slices deli turkey
2 slices cheddar cheese
4 small whole wheat tortillas
1 tablespoon mustard
(optional)

2
SERVINGS

5 MINS
PERP TIME

00 MINS
COOK TIME

INSTRUCTIONS

1. Lay each tortilla flat and spread a little mustard in the center if desired.
2. Place a slice of turkey and half a slice of cheddar cheese on each tortilla.
3. Roll up the tortillas tightly and cut them in the middle. Serve immediately.

NUTRITIONAL VALUES (PER SERVING):

Calories: 230, Protein: 14g,
Carbohydrates: 22g, Fat: 10g, Fiber: 3g

DIY Pita Pocket Sandwiches

INGREDIENTS

2 whole wheat pita bread, halved

1/4 cup hummus

1/4 cup cucumber, sliced

1/4 cup cherry tomatoes, halved

1/4 cup shredded lettuce

1/4 cup shredded cooked chicken (optional)

2
SERVINGS

10 MINS
PERP TIME

00 MINS
COOK TIME

INSTRUCTIONS

1. Spread 1 tablespoon of hummus inside each pita half.
2. Stuff the pita halves with cucumber slices, cherry tomatoes, shredded lettuce, and cooked chicken if using.
3. Serve immediately as a DIY sandwich.

NUTRITIONAL VALUES (PER SERVING):

Calories: 260, Protein: 10g,
Carbohydrates: 38g, Fat: 8g, Fiber: 6g

GRILLED CHEESE SANDWICHES

2	5 MINS	5 MINS
SERVINGS	PERP TIME	COOK TIME

INGREDIENTS

4 slices of whole wheat bread
1/2 cup shredded cheddar cheese
2 tablespoons butter, softened
Cookie cutters (optional for fun shapes)

INSTRUCTIONS

1. Butter one side of each slice of bread.
2. Place two slices, buttered side down, in a heated pan. Sprinkle the shredded cheese on top.
3. Place the other two slices of bread on top, buttered side up. Cook for 2-3 minutes per side until golden brown and the cheese is melted.
4. Use cookie cutters to cut the sandwiches, if desired, and serve immediately.

NUTRITIONAL VALUES (PER SERVING):

Calories: 320, Protein: 10g,
Carbohydrates: 30g, Fat: 18g, Fiber: 3g

Chicken Caesar Salad Wraps

INGREDIENTS

2 whole wheat tortillas
1 cup cooked chicken breast, shredded
1/2 cup romaine lettuce, shredded
1/4 cup Caesar dressing
1/4 cup grated Parmesan cheese

2
SERVINGS

10 MINS
PERP TIME

00 MINS
COOK TIME

INSTRUCTIONS

1. In a deep-bottom bowl, mix the cooked chicken, shredded lettuce, Caesar dressing, and Parmesan cheese.
2. Divide the mixture between the two tortillas.
3. Roll up the tortillas and slice them in half. Serve immediately.

NUTRITIONAL VALUES (PER SERVING):

Calories: 320, Protein: 22g,
Carbohydrates: 30g, Fat: 12g, Fiber: 3g

Mini Bagel Pizzas

INGREDIENTS

2 mini whole wheat bagels, halved
1/4 cup pizza sauce
1/2 cup shredded mozzarella cheese
1/4 cup pepperoni slices or other toppings (optional)

2
SERVINGS

5 MINS
PERP TIME

10 MINS
COOK TIME

INSTRUCTIONS

1. Preheat oven to 400°F (200°C).
2. Spread pizza sauce over each bagel half.
3. Top with shredded mozzarella cheese and add pepperoni slices or other toppings.
4. Place the bagels on the paper-arranged baking sheet and bake for 8-10 minutes. Serve warm.

NUTRITIONAL VALUES (PER SERVING):

Calories: 290, Protein: 14g,
Carbohydrates: 36g, Fat: 10g, Fiber: 3g

44

Taco Salad Bowls

INGREDIENTS

2 small whole wheat tortillas
1/2 cup ground beef or turkey
(cooked)
1/4 cup shredded lettuce
1/4 cup diced tomatoes
1/4 cup shredded cheddar
cheese
2 tablespoons sour cream or
salsa

2
SERVINGS

10 MINS
PERP TIME

5 MINS
COOK TIME

INSTRUCTIONS

1. Preheat oven to 400°F (200°C). Place the tortillas in oven-safe bowls and press to form a bowl shape. Bake for 5-7 minutes until crispy.
2. Fill each tortilla bowl with ground beef or turkey, lettuce, tomatoes, and cheese.
3. Put sour cream or salsa on top and serve immediately.

NUTRITIONAL VALUES (PER SERVING):

Calories: 350, Protein: 18g,
Carbohydrates: 32g, Fat: 18g, Fiber: 4g

HAM AND CHEESE PINWHEELS

INGREDIENTS

4 small whole wheat tortillas
4 slices of deli ham
4 slices of cheddar cheese
2 tablespoons cream cheese, softened

2
SERVINGS

5 MINS
PERP TIME

00 MINS
COOK TIME

INSTRUCTIONS

1. Spread cream cheese (a thin layer) over each tortilla.
2. Place the ham slice and a slice of cheese on each tortilla.
3. Roll up the tortillas tightly. Slice them into pinwheels. Serve immediately.

NUTRITIONAL VALUES (PER SERVING):

Calories: 270, Protein: 15g,
Carbohydrates: 28g, Fat: 12g, Fiber: 3g

Tuna Salad Lettuce Wraps

INGREDIENTS

1 can (5 oz) tuna, drained
2 tablespoons mayonnaise or
Greek yogurt
1 tablespoon mustard
1/4 cup diced celery
1/4 cup diced red bell pepper
4 large lettuce leaves (romaine
or iceberg)
Salt and pepper to taste

2
SERVINGS

10 MINS
PERP TIME

00 MINS
COOK TIME

INSTRUCTIONS

1. In a deep-bottom bowl, mix the tuna, mayonnaise or yogurt, mustard, celery, bell pepper, salt, and pepper.
2. Spoon the tuna salad onto the center of each lettuce leaf.
3. Roll up the lettuce leaves and serve immediately as wraps.

NUTRITIONAL VALUES (PER SERVING):

Calories: 180, Protein: 18g,
Carbohydrates: 4g, Fat: 10g, Fiber: 1g

Hummus and Veggie Sandwich

INGREDIENTS

4 slices whole wheat bread
1/4 cup hummus
1/4 cup cucumber slices
1/4 cup shredded carrots
1/4 cup sliced bell peppers
1/4 cup spinach leaves

2
SERVINGS

5 MINS
PERP TIME

00 MINS
COOK TIME

INSTRUCTIONS

1. Spread two tbsp hummus on each slice of bread.
2. Layer the cucumber, carrots, bell peppers, and spinach on two of the bread slices.
3. Top with the other bread slices, hummus side down, and press gently. Cut the sandwiches in half and serve.

NUTRITIONAL VALUES (PER SERVING):

Calories: 280, Protein: 8g,
Carbohydrates: 40g, Fat: 10g, Fiber: 6g

CREAMY MAC AND CHEESE CUPS

INGREDIENTS

1 cup elbow macaroni
1 tablespoon butter
1 tablespoon flour
1 cup milk
1 1/2 cups shredded cheddar
cheese
Salt and pepper to taste

4
SERVINGS

10 MINS
PERP TIME

15 MINS
COOK TIME

INSTRUCTIONS

1. Preheat oven to 350°F (180°C). Grease a muffin tin. Prepare macaroni according to the steps mentioned in the package guide and drain.
2. Melt one tbsp butter over medium heat. Toss in flour and cook for one minute.
3. Slowly add milk in small portions and cook until it thickens. Toss in the shredded cheese, salt, and crushed pepper until melted and creamy.
4. Mix the cheese sauce with the prepared macaroni and spoon into the muffin cups. Bake for 10-15 minutes until the tops are slightly golden. Let cool slightly before serving.

NUTRITIONAL VALUES (PER SERVING):

Calories: 300, Protein: 12g,
Carbohydrates: 32g, Fat: 15g, Fiber: 1g

49

Pepperoni Pizza Rolls

INGREDIENTS

1 tube refrigerated pizza dough
1/2 cup pizza sauce
1/2 cup shredded mozzarella cheese
1/4 cup pepperoni slices
1 tablespoon olive oil (optional)

2
SERVINGS

10 MINS
PERP TIME

12 MINS
COOK TIME

INSTRUCTIONS

1. Preheat oven to 375°F (190°C).
2. Roll out the pizza dough, then spread pizza sauce evenly over the surface.
3. Sprinkle with shredded cheese over the pizza sauce layer and top with pepperoni slices.
4. Roll up the dough into a log form and slice it into 1-inch pieces.
5. Place the rolls on a baking sheet and brush with olive oil if desired.
6. Bake for 10-12 minutes until golden brown. Serve warm.

NUTRITIONAL VALUES (PER SERVING):

Calories: 320, Protein: 14g,
Carbohydrates: 36g, Fat: 14g, Fiber: 2g

Sweet and Savory Chicken Skewers

2
SERVINGS

15 MINS
PERP TIME

10 MINS
COOK TIME

INGREDIENTS

1 chicken breast, cut into bite-sized pieces
2 tablespoons honey
2 tablespoons soy sauce
1 tablespoon olive oil
1 bell pepper, cut into chunks
1 small red onion, cut into chunks
Wooden skewers soaked in water

INSTRUCTIONS

1. In a deep-bottom bowl, mix honey, soy sauce, and olive oil. Add meat pieces and marinate for 10 minutes (at least).
2. Thread the meat, bell pepper, and onion onto the skewers.
3. Heat a grill pan or outdoor grill.
4. Cook the skewers for 8-10 minutes until the chicken is cooked through. Serve warm.

NUTRITIONAL VALUES (PER SERVING):

Calories: 250, Protein: 24g,
Carbohydrates: 20g, Fat: 8g, Fiber: 2g

Veggie-Packed Pasta Salad

2
SERVINGS

10 MINS
PERP TIME

10 MINS
COOK TIME

INGREDIENTS

1 cup whole wheat pasta (penne or rotini)
1/4 cup cherry tomatoes, halved
1/4 cup diced cucumber
1/4 cup bell peppers, diced
1/4 cup shredded carrots
2 tablespoons Italian dressing
1 tablespoon grated Parmesan cheese (optional)

INSTRUCTIONS

1. Cook the pasta according to package instructions. Drain and let cool.
2. In a deep-bottom bowl, combine the cooled pasta, cherry tomatoes, cucumber, bell peppers, and carrots.
3. Drizzle Italian dressing and toss to coat.
4. Spread cheese on top if desired, and serve chilled.

NUTRITIONAL VALUES (PER SERVING):

Calories: 240, Protein: 7g,
Carbohydrates: 38g, Fat: 7g, Fiber: 6g

Tomato Basil Grilled Cheese

INGREDIENTS

4 slices of whole wheat bread
4 slices of mozzarella cheese
1 small tomato, sliced
4-5 fresh basil leaves
2 tablespoons butter, softened

| **2**
SERVINGS | **5 MINS**
PERP TIME | **5 MINS**
COOK TIME |

INSTRUCTIONS

1. Butter one side of each slice of bread.
2. Place two slices of bread, buttered side down, in a heated pan.
3. Top with mozzarella cheese, tomato slices, and basil leaves.
4. Place the other two slices of bread on top, buttered side up. Cook for 2-3 minutes on one side until golden brown and the cheese is melted.
5. Slice in half and serve warm.

NUTRITIONAL VALUES (PER SERVING):

Calories: 330, Protein: 14g,
Carbohydrates: 34g, Fat: 16g, Fiber: 4g

Chicken and Avocado Sandwiches

INGREDIENTS

2 whole wheat sandwich rolls
or bread slices
1 cooked chicken breast,
shredded
1 avocado, mashed
1 tablespoon mayonnaise or
Greek yogurt (optional)
1/4 cup baby spinach leaves
Salt and pepper to taste

2
SERVINGS

10 MINS
PERP TIME

00 MINS
COOK TIME

INSTRUCTIONS

1. In a small, deep-bottom bowl, mix the mashed avocado with mayonnaise or yogurt if using. Season with salt and pepper.
2. Spread the avocado mixture on the sandwich rolls or bread slices.
3. Add the shredded chicken and spinach leaves on top.
4. Close the sandwiches and serve immediately.

NUTRITIONAL VALUES (PER SERVING):

Calories: 350, Protein: 24g,
Carbohydrates: 32g, Fat: 15g, Fiber: 8g

Meatball Subs with Marinara Sauce

2	10 MINS	15 MINS
SERVINGS	PERP TIME	COOK TIME

INGREDIENTS

4 small meatballs (homemade or store-bought)
1/2 cup marinara sauce
2 small sandwich rolls
1/4 cup shredded mozzarella cheese

INSTRUCTIONS

1. Preheat oven to 350°F (180°C).
2. Heat the meatballs in marinara sauce over medium heat.
3. Place the meatballs in the sandwich rolls and spoon marinara sauce over the top.
4. Sprinkle cheese on the meatballs
5. top. Place the subs on a baking sheet.
6. Bake for 5-7 minutes until cheese melts thoroughly. Serve warm.

NUTRITIONAL VALUES (PER SERVING):

Calories: 400, Protein: 20g,
Carbohydrates: 35g, Fat: 18g, Fiber: 3g

Snack Attack

Fruit and Cheese Kabobs

INGREDIENTS

1/2 cup strawberries, hulled and halved
1/2 cup grapes
1/2 cup cubed cheddar cheese
1/2 cup pineapple chunks
Wooden or reusable skewers

2
SERVINGS

10 MINS
PERP TIME

00 MINS
COOK TIME

INSTRUCTIONS

1. Thread the fruit and cheese cubes onto the skewers, alternating between strawberries, grapes, cheddar cheese, and pineapple.
2. Repeat until all the ingredients are used.
3. Serve immediately.

NUTRITIONAL VALUES (PER SERVING):

Calories: 200, Protein: 8g,
Carbohydrates: 28g, Fat: 8g, Fiber: 3g

Chicken and Avocado Sandwiches

2
SERVINGS

10 MINS
PERP TIME

00 MINS
COOK TIME

INGREDIENTS

2 whole wheat sandwich rolls
or bread slices
1 cooked chicken breast,
shredded
1 avocado, mashed
1 tablespoon mayonnaise or
Greek yogurt (optional)
1/4 cup baby spinach leaves
Salt and pepper to taste

INSTRUCTIONS

1. In a small, deep-bottom bowl, mix the mashed avocado with mayonnaise or yogurt if using. Season with salt and pepper.
2. Spread the avocado mixture on the sandwich rolls or bread slices.
3. Add the shredded chicken and spinach leaves on top.
4. Close the sandwiches and serve immediately.

NUTRITIONAL VALUES (PER SERVING):

Calories: 350, Protein: 24g,
Carbohydrates: 32g, Fat: 15g, Fiber: 8g

Sweet and Salty Popcorn Mix

INGREDIENTS

4 cups popped popcorn
1/4 cup pretzels, broken into pieces
1/4 cup dried cranberries
2 tablespoons mini chocolate chips
1/4 teaspoon salt

2	5 MINS	5 MINS
SERVINGS	PERP TIME	COOK TIME

INSTRUCTIONS

1. In a deep-bottom bowl, combine the popped popcorn, pretzels, dried cranberries, and mini chocolate chips.
2. Sprinkle with salt and toss to combine.
3. Serve immediately.

NUTRITIONAL VALUES (PER SERVING):

Calories: 150, Protein: 3g,
Carbohydrates: 25g, Fat: 5g, Fiber: 3g

Apple Nachos with Peanut Butter Drizzle

INGREDIENTS

2 medium apples, cored and sliced
2 tablespoons peanut butter, melted
1 tablespoon mini chocolate chips
1 tablespoon granola (optional)

2
SERVINGS

5 MINS
PERP TIME

00 MINS
COOK TIME

INSTRUCTIONS

1. Arrange apple slices on the serving shallow plate in a circular pattern.
2. Drizzle melted peanut butter over the arranged slices.
3. Sprinkle with mini chocolate chips and granola if using.
4. Serve immediately as a fun, healthy snack.

NUTRITIONAL VALUES (PER SERVING):

Calories: 220, Protein: 4g,
Carbohydrates: 38g, Fat: 8g, Fiber: 5g

Sweet Mini Veggie Pizzas on English Muffins

2
SERVINGS

5 MINS
PERP TIME

10 MINS
COOK TIME

INGREDIENTS

2 whole wheat English
muffins, halved
1/4 cup pizza sauce
1/2 cup shredded mozzarella
cheese
1/4 cup diced bell peppers
1/4 cup sliced black olives
(optional)
1/4 cup sliced mushrooms
(optional)

INSTRUCTIONS

1. Preheat oven to 400°F (200°C).
2. Spread pizza sauce evenly over each half of the English muffin.
3. Sprinkle with shredded mozzarella cheese, then add the diced
   bell peppers, olives, and mushrooms.
4. Place the mini pizzas on the paper-arranged baking sheet and
   bake for 8-10 minutes. Serve warm.

NUTRITIONAL VALUES (PER SERVING):

Calories: 280, Protein: 12g,
Carbohydrates: 34g, Fat: 10g, Fiber: 6g

Cheesy Garlic Breadsticks

INGREDIENTS

4 small slices of French bread or baguette

2 tablespoons butter, melted

1/2 teaspoon garlic powder

1/2 cup shredded mozzarella cheese

1 tablespoon grated Parmesan cheese

1 tablespoon chopped parsley (optional)

2	**5 MINS**	**10 MINS**
SERVINGS	PERP TIME	COOK TIME

INSTRUCTIONS

1. Preheat oven to 375°F (190°C).
2. Arrange the bread slices on the parchment paper-arranged baking sheet.
3. In a small, deep-bottom bowl, mix the melted butter with garlic powder and brush it over the bread slices.
4. Sprinkle shredded mozzarella cheese, Parmesan, and parsley on top of each slice.
5. Bake for 8-10 minutes. Serve warm.

NUTRITIONAL VALUES (PER SERVING):

Calories: 230, Protein: 10g,
Carbohydrates: 25g, Fat: 10g, Fiber: 2g

Peanut Butter and Banana Sushi Rolls

INGREDIENTS

2 slices whole wheat bread
2 tablespoons peanut butter
1 banana, peeled
1 tablespoon honey (optional)

2
SERVINGS

5 MINS
PERP TIME

00 MINS
COOK TIME

INSTRUCTIONS

1. Trim the bread slices' crusts and flatten them with a rolling pin.
2. Spread peanut butter evenly over each slice of bread.
3. Place a whole banana on each slice and roll the bread tightly around it.
4. Slice into 1-inch "sushi" rolls and drizzle with honey if desired. Serve immediately.

NUTRITIONAL VALUES (PER SERVING):

Calories: 280, Protein: 8g,
Carbohydrates: 40g, Fat: 12g, Fiber: 6g

ANTS ON A LOG

INGREDIENTS

4 celery stalks
4 tablespoons peanut butter
1/4 cup raisins

2
SERVINGS

5 MINS
PERP TIME

00 MINS
COOK TIME

INSTRUCTIONS

1. Spread peanut butter into the hollow of each celery stalk.
2. Place raisins on top of the peanut butter, spacing them out like "ants" on a log.
3. Serve immediately as a fun and healthy snack.

NUTRITIONAL VALUES (PER SERVING):

Calories: 200, Protein: 5g,
Carbohydrates: 25g, Fat: 10g, Fiber: 4g

Strawberry Yogurt Parfait Cups

2
SERVINGS

5 MINS
PERP TIME

00 MINS
COOK TIME

INGREDIENTS

1 cup plain Greek yogurt
1/2 cup fresh strawberries, sliced
1/4 cup granola
1 tablespoon honey (optional)

INSTRUCTIONS

1. In two small cups, layer 1/4 cup of Greek yogurt at the bottom of each.
2. Put the sliced strawberries layer, followed by 1 tablespoon of granola.
3. Repeat the layers with the remaining yogurt, strawberries, and granola.
4. Drizzle honey if desired, and serve immediately.

NUTRITIONAL VALUES (PER SERVING):

Calories: 180, Protein: 10g,
Carbohydrates: 25g, Fat: 5g, Fiber: 3g

Cheese and Crackers Fun Faces

INGREDIENTS

8 whole grain crackers
4 slices of cheddar cheese, cut into circles to fit the crackers
4 cucumber slices
4 cherry tomatoes, halved
4 olives, halved

2
SERVINGS

5 MINS
PERP TIME

00 MINS
COOK TIME

INSTRUCTIONS

1. Place a slice of cheddar cheese on top of each cracker.
2. Use the cucumber slices, cherry tomatoes, and olives to create fun faces on the cheese (e.g., cucumber for eyes, tomatoes for a nose, and olives for a mouth).
3. Serve immediately as a playful snack.

NUTRITIONAL VALUES (PER SERVING):

Calories: 150, Protein: 6g,
Carbohydrates: 16g, Fat: 8g, Fiber: 2g

Frozen Grapes and Yogurt Bites

2
SERVINGS

5 MINS
PERP TIME

00 MINS
COOK TIME

INGREDIENTS

1 cup seedless grapes
1/2 cup plain Greek yogurt
1 tablespoon honey (optional)

INSTRUCTIONS

1. Dip each grape into the Greek yogurt, ensuring it's fully coated.
2. Place the yogurt-covered grapes on a parchment paper-arranged baking sheet.
3. Freeze for 1-2 hours until the yogurt is firm.
4. Drizzle with honey if desired and serve as a refreshing snack.

NUTRITIONAL VALUES (PER SERVING):

Calories: 120, Protein: 5g,
Carbohydrates: 24g, Fat: 1g, Fiber: 2g

Cinnamon Apple Chips

INGREDIENTS

2 apples, thinly sliced
1 teaspoon cinnamon

2
SERVINGS

10 MINS
PERP TIME

1 HOUR
COOK TIME

INSTRUCTIONS

1. Preheat oven to 225°F (110°C). Arrange the baking sheet with parchment paper.
2. Arrange the apple slices in one layer (don't overlap) on the parchment paper-arranged baking sheet.
3. Sprinkle cinnamon powder evenly over the apple slices.
4. Bake for 1 hour, turning the slices halfway through, until the apples are crispy.
5. Let cool and serve as a healthy snack.

NUTRITIONAL VALUES (PER SERVING):

Calories: 90, Protein: 0g, Carbohydrates:
25g, Fat: 0g, Fiber: 4g

Veggie Sticks with Ranch Dip

INGREDIENTS

1/2 cup carrot sticks
1/2 cup cucumber sticks
1/2 cup celery sticks
1/4 cup ranch dressing (store-bought or homemade)

2
SERVINGS

5 MINS
PERP TIME

00 MINS
COOK TIME

INSTRUCTIONS

1. Arrange the carrot, cucumber, and celery sticks on a plate.
2. Serve with ranch dressing for dipping.
3. Enjoy as a refreshing snack!

NUTRITIONAL VALUES (PER SERVING):

Calories: 120, Protein: 1g,
Carbohydrates: 12g, Fat: 8g, Fiber: 3g

Zucchini Chips with Marinara Sauce

INGREDIENTS

1 medium zucchini, thinly sliced
1 tablespoon olive oil
1/4 teaspoon salt
1/4 cup marinara sauce (for dipping)

2
SERVINGS

10 MINS
PERP TIME

15 MINS
COOK TIME

INSTRUCTIONS

1. Preheat oven to 400°F (200°C). Arrange the baking sheet with parchment paper.
2. Toss the zucchini slices with one tbsp oil and salt.
3. Arrange the slices in one layer (don't overlap) on the parchment paper-arranged baking sheet.
4. Bake for 12-15 minutes. Serve with marinara sauce for dipping.

NUTRITIONAL VALUES (PER SERVING):

Calories: 100, Protein: 2g,
Carbohydrates: 8g, Fat: 7g, Fiber: 2g

TRAIL MIX WITH NUTS AND DRIED FRUIT

INGREDIENTS

1/4 cup almonds

1/4 cup cashews

1/4 cup raisins

1/4 cup dried cranberries

2 tablespoons mini chocolate chips (optional)

2
SERVINGS

5 MINS
PERP TIME

00 MINS
COOK TIME

INSTRUCTIONS

1. In a small, deep-bottom bowl, combine the almonds, cashews, raisins, dried cranberries, and chocolate chips if using.
2. Mix well and divide into portions.
3. Serve as a quick, portable snack.

NUTRITIONAL VALUES (PER SERVING):

Calories: 250, Protein: 6g,
Carbohydrates: 30g, Fat: 12g, Fiber: 4g

Cucumber Sandwich Bites

INGREDIENTS

1 cucumber, sliced into rounds
1/4 cup cream cheese
1 tablespoon fresh dill, chopped
Salt and pepper to taste

2
SERVINGS

5 MINS
PERP TIME

00 MINS
COOK TIME

INSTRUCTIONS

1. Spread a small amount of cream cheese on each cucumber round.
2. Sprinkle with chopped dill and powder it with salt and crushed pepper to taste.
3. Serve immediately as a refreshing sandwich bites.

NUTRITIONAL VALUES (PER SERVING):

Calories: 100, Protein: 2g,
Carbohydrates: 4g, Fat: 8g, Fiber: 1g

Watermelon and Feta Skewers

2
SERVINGS

10 MINS
PERP TIME

00 MINS
COOK TIME

INGREDIENTS

1 cup watermelon, cubed
1/2 cup feta cheese, cubed
6-8 fresh mint leaves
Wooden or reusable skewers

INSTRUCTIONS

1. Thread a cube of watermelon, a cube of feta, and a mint leaf onto each skewer.
2. Repeat the process until all ingredients are used.
3. Serve immediately as a refreshing and light snack.

NUTRITIONAL VALUES (PER SERVING):

Calories: 130, Protein: 4g,
Carbohydrates: 15g, Fat: 7g, Fiber: 1g

Homemade Granola Bars

4	**10 MINS**	**00 MINS**
SERVINGS	PERP TIME	COOK TIME

INGREDIENTS

1 1/2 cups rolled oats
1/4 cup peanut butter
1/4 cup honey
1/4 cup mini chocolate chips
(optional)
1/4 cup chopped nuts
(optional)

INSTRUCTIONS

1. In a microwave-safe bowl, melt the peanut butter and honey together until smooth (about 30 seconds).
2. In a deep-bottom bowl, mix the oats, chocolate chips, and nuts (if using).
3. Drop peanut butter honey mixture over the oats and stir until well combined.
4. Press the mixture firmly toward the greased or parchment paper-arranged baking dish.
5. Refrigerate for one hour (at least) before cutting into bars.

NUTRITIONAL VALUES (PER SERVING):

Calories: 220, Protein: 5g,
Carbohydrates: 30g, Fat: 9g, Fiber: 3g

CARROT AND CUCUMBER ROLL-UPS

INGREDIENTS

1 large carrot, peeled into thin
ribbons
1 cucumber, peeled into thin
ribbons
1/4 cup hummus
2 tablespoons chopped
parsley (optional)

2
SERVINGS

5 MINS
PERP TIME

00 MINS
COOK TIME

INSTRUCTIONS

1. Lay the carrot and cucumber ribbons flat and spread a small
    amount of hummus on each.
2. Roll the ribbons tightly and secure with a toothpick if needed.
3. Spread chopped parsley if desired, and serve immediately.

NUTRITIONAL VALUES (PER SERVING):

Calories: 80, Protein: 2g, Carbohydrates:
10g, Fat: 4g, Fiber: 3g

Apple Slices with Cinnamon Yogurt Dip

2
SERVINGS

5 MINS
PERP TIME

00 MINS
COOK TIME

INGREDIENTS

2 apples, cored and sliced
1/2 cup plain Greek yogurt
1 tablespoon honey
1/2 teaspoon cinnamon

INSTRUCTIONS

1. In a small, deep-bottom bowl, mix the Greek yogurt, honey, and cinnamon until smooth.
2. Arrange the apple slices on a shallow plate and serve with the cinnamon yogurt dip on the side.

NUTRITIONAL VALUES (PER SERVING):

Calories: 160, Protein: 5g,
Carbohydrates: 34g, Fat: 1g, Fiber: 5g

DINNER TIME DELIGHTS

Easy Cheesy Mac and Cheese

INGREDIENTS

1 cup elbow macaroni
1 tablespoon butter
1 tablespoon all-purpose flour
1 cup milk
1 1/2 cups shredded cheddar cheese
Salt and pepper to taste

2
SERVINGS

5 MINS
PERP TIME

15 MINS
COOK TIME

INSTRUCTIONS

1. Cook the macaroni according to the steps mentioned in the package guidelines. Drain and set aside.
2. Melt the butter over a medium stove flame. Toss in flour and cook for 1 minute.
3. Slowly add milk in small portions and cook until the sauce thickens about 3-4 minutes.
4. Toss in the shredded cheese until fully melted and creamy. Season with salt and pepper.
5. Add prepared macaroni to the cheese sauce and stir to coat. Serve warmly.

NUTRITIONAL VALUES (PER SERVING):

Calories: 400, Protein: 16g,
Carbohydrates: 48g, Fat: 18g, Fiber: 2g

CRISPY CHICKEN TENDERS

INGREDIENTS

1 chicken breast, cut into strips
1/2 cup breadcrumbs
1/4 cup grated Parmesan cheese
1 egg, beaten
1/4 teaspoon salt
1/4 teaspoon pepper
1 tablespoon olive oil

2 SERVINGS **10 MINS** PERP TIME **15 MINS** COOK TIME

INSTRUCTIONS

1. Preheat oven to 400°F (200°C). Arrange the baking sheet with parchment paper.
2. In a deep-bottom dish, mix the breadcrumbs, Parmesan cheese, salt, and crushed pepper.
3. Dip each meat strip into the beaten egg, then coat it with the breadcrumb mixture.
4. Arrange the chicken strips on the parchment paper-arranged baking sheet and drizzle with olive oil.
5. Bake for 12-15 minutes or until golden brown and crispy. Serve with your favorite dipping sauce.

NUTRITIONAL VALUES (PER SERVING):

Calories: 320, Protein: 28g,
Carbohydrates: 20g, Fat: 14g, Fiber: 1g

Baked Mini Meatball Sliders

INGREDIENTS

1/2 pound ground beef or turkey
1/4 cup breadcrumbs
1 egg
1/4 cup grated Parmesan cheese
1/4 cup marinara sauce
4 small slider buns
1/4 cup shredded mozzarella cheese

2
SERVINGS

10 MINS
PERP TIME

15 MINS
COOK TIME

INSTRUCTIONS

1. Preheat oven to 375°F (190°C).
2. Mix the ground meat, breadcrumbs, egg, and Parmesan cheese in a deep-bottom bowl. Form the mixture into small meatballs.
3. Arrange the meatballs on the paper-arranged baking sheet and bake for 12-15 minutes.
4. Slice the slider buns and place a meatball on each bun. Top with marinara sauce and shredded mozzarella.
5. Bake the assembled sliders for 5 minutes or until the cheese is melted. Serve warm.

NUTRITIONAL VALUES (PER SERVING):

Calories: 350, Protein: 22g,
Carbohydrates: 28g, Fat: 15g, Fiber: 2g

Veggie-Packed Pasta Salad

INGREDIENTS

1 cup whole wheat pasta
(penne or rotini)
1/4 cup cherry tomatoes,
halved
1/4 cup diced cucumber
1/4 cup shredded carrots
1/4 cup chopped bell peppers
2 tablespoons Italian dressing
1 tablespoon grated Parmesan
cheese (optional)

2
SERVINGS

10 MINS
PERP TIME

10 MINS
COOK TIME

INSTRUCTIONS

1. Cook the pasta according to the steps mentioned in the package guidelines. Drain and let cool.
2. In a deep-bottom bowl, combine the cooled pasta, cherry tomatoes, cucumber, carrots, and bell peppers.
3. Drizzle Italian dressing and toss to coat.
4. Sprinkle with shredded cheese on top if desired, and serve chilled.

NUTRITIONAL VALUES (PER SERVING):

Calories: 260, Protein: 8g,
Carbohydrates: 40g, Fat: 8g, Fiber: 6g

Homemade Chicken Nuggets

INGREDIENTS

1 chicken breast, cut into bite-
sized pieces
1/2 cup breadcrumbs
1/4 cup grated Parmesan
cheese
1 egg, beaten
1/4 teaspoon salt
1/4 teaspoon pepper
1 tablespoon olive oil

2	**10 MINS**	**12 MINS**
SERVINGS	PERP TIME	COOK TIME

INSTRUCTIONS

1. Preheat oven to 400°F (200°C). Arrange the baking sheet with parchment paper.
2. In a deep-bottom dish, mix the breadcrumbs, Parmesan cheese, salt, and pepper.
3. Dip each meat piece into the beaten egg, then coat it with the breadcrumb mixture.
4. Arrange the chicken pieces on the parchment paper-arranged baking sheet and drizzle with olive oil.
5. Bake for 10-12 minutes or until golden brown and cooked through. Serve with your favorite dipping sauce.

NUTRITIONAL VALUES (PER SERVING):

Calories: 300, Protein: 26g,
Carbohydrates: 18g, Fat: 14g, Fiber: 1g

Cheese-Stuffed Pasta Shells

INGREDIENTS

8 large pasta shells
1/2 cup ricotta cheese
1/4 cup shredded mozzarella cheese
1/4 cup grated Parmesan cheese
1/2 teaspoon dried oregano
1 cup marinara sauce

2
SERVINGS

10 MINS
PERP TIME

20 MINS
COOK TIME

INSTRUCTIONS

1. Preheat oven to 375°F (190°C). Cook the pasta shells according to the steps mentioned in the package guidelines, then drain and set aside.
2. In a deep-bottom bowl, mix the ricotta, mozzarella, Parmesan, and oregano.
3. Fill pasta shells with the cheese mixture and place them in a baking dish.
4. Drop marinara sauce over the stuffed shells.
5. Bake for 15-20 minutes. Serve warm.

NUTRITIONAL VALUES (PER SERVING):

Calories: 350, Protein: 18g,
Carbohydrates: 36g, Fat: 16g, Fiber: 4g

BBQ Chicken Drumsticks

INGREDIENTS

4 chicken drumsticks
1/2 cup BBQ sauce
1 tablespoon olive oil
Salt and pepper to taste

2
SERVINGS

10 MINS
PERP TIME

25 MINS
COOK TIME

INSTRUCTIONS

1. Preheat oven to 400°F (200°C). Arrange the baking sheet with parchment paper.
2. Drizzle olive oil over the chicken drumsticks and season with salt and pepper.
3. Place the drumsticks on the parchment paper-arranged baking sheet and bake for 20 minutes.
4. After 20 minutes, brush the BBQ sauce onto the drumsticks and bake for an additional 5 minutes or until the sauce is caramelized.
5. Serve with extra BBQ sauce if desired.

NUTRITIONAL VALUES (PER SERVING):

Calories: 300, Protein: 25g,
Carbohydrates: 12g, Fat: 16g, Fiber: 0g

Spaghetti with Hidden Veggie Sauce

INGREDIENTS

1 cup whole wheat spaghetti
1/2 cup marinara sauce
1/4 cup finely grated zucchini
1/4 cup finely grated carrots
1/4 cup diced bell peppers
1 tablespoon olive oil
Salt and pepper to taste
Grated Parmesan cheese
(optional)

2
SERVINGS

10 MINS
PERP TIME

15 MINS
COOK TIME

INSTRUCTIONS

1. Cook the spaghetti according to the steps mentioned in the package guidelines. Drain and set aside.
2. Heat one tbsp oil over medium stove flame and sauté the grated zucchini, carrots, and bell peppers for 3-4 minutes until soft.
3. Add marinara sauce and wait to simmer for 5 minutes. Season with salt and pepper.
4. Toss the cooked spaghetti with the veggie-packed marinara sauce.
5. Serve with grated Parmesan cheese if desired.

NUTRITIONAL VALUES (PER SERVING):

Calories: 280, Protein: 10g,
Carbohydrates: 46g, Fat: 8g, Fiber: 7g

Mini Turkey Meatloaves

INGREDIENTS

1/2 pound ground turkey
1/4 cup breadcrumbs
1 egg
1/4 cup grated Parmesan cheese
1/4 cup ketchup
1 teaspoon garlic powder
Salt and pepper to taste

2
SERVINGS

10 MINS
PERP TIME

20 MINS
COOK TIME

INSTRUCTIONS

1. Preheat oven to 375°F (190°C). Grease a muffin tin.
2. In a deep-bottom bowl, mix the ground turkey, breadcrumbs, egg, Parmesan, garlic powder, salt, and pepper.
3. Divide the mixture into four sections and press each portion into a muffin cup.
4. Top each mini meatloaf with a spoonful of ketchup.
5. Bake for 20 minutes or until the meatloaves are fully cooked. Serve warm.

NUTRITIONAL VALUES (PER SERVING):

Calories: 280, Protein: 28g,
Carbohydrates: 18g, Fat: 10g, Fiber: 1g

Pizza Stuffed Peppers

INGREDIENTS

2 bell peppers, halved and seeds removed

1/2 cup pizza sauce

1/2 cup shredded mozzarella cheese

1/4 cup mini pepperoni slices

1 tablespoon grated Parmesan cheese

1 teaspoon Italian seasoning

2
SERVINGS

10 MINS
PERP TIME

20 MINS
COOK TIME

INSTRUCTIONS

1. Preheat oven to 375°F (190°C).
2. Arrange bell pepper halves in a baking dish.
3. Fill each bell pepper half with pizza sauce and top with mozzarella cheese, mini pepperoni, Parmesan, and Italian seasoning.
4. Bake for 15-20 minutes until the peppers get tender. Serve warm.

NUTRITIONAL VALUES (PER SERVING):

Calories: 220, Protein: 12g,
Carbohydrates: 16g, Fat: 12g, Fiber: 4g

Simple Shrimp Stir-Fry

INGREDIENTS

1/2 pound shrimp, peeled and deveined
1/2 cup broccoli florets
1/2 cup bell peppers, sliced
1/2 cup carrots, sliced
2 tablespoons soy sauce
1 tablespoon olive oil
1 teaspoon honey
1/2 teaspoon garlic powder

2
SERVINGS

10 MINS
PERP TIME

10 MINS
COOK TIME

INSTRUCTIONS

1. Heat one tbsp oil over medium stove flame. Add shrimp and cook for three minutes until they turn pink. Remove from the pan and set aside.
2. Use the same pan and add the broccoli, bell peppers, and carrots. Stir-fry for 5-7 minutes until tender.
3. In a small, deep-bottom bowl, mix the soy sauce, honey, and garlic powder.
4. Add shrimp back into the pan and pour the sauce over the mixture. Stir well and cook for another 2 minutes.
5. Serve immediately over rice or noodles.

NUTRITIONAL VALUES (PER SERVING):

Calories: 230, Protein: 22g,
Carbohydrates: 12g, Fat: 9g, Fiber: 3g

Baked Fish Sticks with Tartar Sauce

	2	10 MINS	15 MINS
	SERVINGS	PERP TIME	COOK TIME

INGREDIENTS

1/2 lb. white fish fillets (cod),
cut into strips

1/2 cup breadcrumbs

1/4 cup grated Parmesan
cheese

1 egg, beaten

1/4 teaspoon salt

1/4 teaspoon pepper

1 tablespoon olive oil

Tartar Sauce Ingredients:

1/4 cup mayonnaise

1 tablespoon pickle relish

1 teaspoon lemon juice

INSTRUCTIONS

1. Preheat oven to 400°F (200°C). Arrange the baking sheet with parchment paper. In a deep-bottom dish, mix the breadcrumbs, Parmesan cheese, salt, and pepper.

2. Dip each fish strip into the beaten egg, then coat it with the breadcrumb mixture.

3. Arrange the fish strips on the parchment paper-arranged baking sheet and drizzle with olive oil.

4. Bake for 12-15 minutes.

5. For the tartar sauce, mix the mayonnaise, pickle relish, and lemon juice in a small, deep-bottom bowl. Serve the fish sticks with tartar sauce on the side.

NUTRITIONAL VALUES (PER SERVING):

Calories: 320, Protein: 30g,
Carbohydrates: 20g, Fat: 14g, Fiber: 1g

MEATBALL AND VEGGIE SKEWERS

INGREDIENTS

8 small meatballs (homemade or store-bought)
1/2 cup cherry tomatoes
1/2 cup bell peppers, cut into chunks
1/2 cup zucchini, sliced
Wooden skewers soaked in water

2	**10 MINS**	**15 MINS**
SERVINGS	PERP TIME	COOK TIME

INSTRUCTIONS

1. Preheat oven to 375°F (190°C). You can burn the grill.
2. Thread the meatballs, cherry tomatoes, bell peppers, and zucchini onto the skewers.
3. Arrange the skewers on a baking sheet or grill and cook for 12-15 minutes, turning from time to time, until the meatballs are fully cooked and the veggies are tender.
4. Serve with dipping sauce and rice.

NUTRITIONAL VALUES (PER SERVING):

Calories: 300, Protein: 22g,
Carbohydrates: 15g, Fat: 16g, Fiber: 3g

Cheesy Baked Ziti

INGREDIENTS

1 cup ziti pasta
1/2 cup marinara sauce
1/2 cup ricotta cheese
1/2 cup shredded mozzarella cheese
1/4 cup grated Parmesan cheese
1 teaspoon Italian seasoning

2
SERVINGS

10 MINS
PERP TIME

20 MINS
COOK TIME

INSTRUCTIONS

1. Preheat oven to 375°F (190°C).
2. Cook the ziti according to the steps mentioned in the package guidelines, then drain.
3. In a deep-bottom bowl, mix the cooked ziti with the marinara sauce, ricotta cheese, and Italian seasoning.
4. Transfer the mixture to the paper-arranged baking dish. Top with mozzarella and Parmesan cheese.
5. Bake for 15-20 minutes. Serve warm.

NUTRITIONAL VALUES (PER SERVING):

Calories: 420, Protein: 18g,
Carbohydrates: 50g, Fat: 18g, Fiber: 4g

Chicken Alfredo Pasta Bake

INGREDIENTS

1 chicken breast, cooked and shredded
1 cup penne pasta
1/2 cup Alfredo sauce
1/4 cup shredded mozzarella cheese
1/4 cup grated Parmesan cheese
1/2 teaspoon garlic powder

2
SERVINGS

10 MINS
PERP TIME

20 MINS
COOK TIME

INSTRUCTIONS

1. Preheat oven to 375°F (190°C).
2. Cook the penne pasta according to the steps mentioned in the package guidelines, then drain.
3. In a deep-bottom bowl, mix the cooked pasta with shredded chicken, Alfredo sauce, and garlic powder.
4. Transfer the mixture to a shallow baking sheet. Top with mozzarella and Parmesan cheese.
5. Bake for 15-20 minutes. Serve warm.

NUTRITIONAL VALUES (PER SERVING):

Calories: 450, Protein: 30g,
Carbohydrates: 40g, Fat: 20g, Fiber: 2g

Veggie and Cheese Stuffed Potatoes

2
SERVINGS

10 MINS
PERP TIME

15 MINS
COOK TIME

INGREDIENTS

2 large potatoes
1/2 cup broccoli florets, steamed
1/4 cup bell peppers, diced
1/4 cup shredded cheddar cheese
1/4 cup sour cream (optional)
Salt and pepper to taste

INSTRUCTIONS

1. Pierce the potatoes with a fork. Put in the microwave for 8-10 minutes, then bake at 400°F (200°C) for 45 minutes in the oven until tender.
2. Slice the prepared potatoes in half and scoop out some of the potato flesh, creating a hollow center.
3. In a deep-bottom bowl, mix the steamed broccoli, bell peppers, and shredded cheddar cheese. Season with salt and pepper.
4. Spoon the veggie and cheese mixture into the hollowed-out potatoes. Microwave for 1-2 minutes, then bake for 5 minutes. Serve with sour cream if desired.

NUTRITIONAL VALUES (PER SERVING):

Calories: 260, Protein: 10g,
Carbohydrates: 48g, Fat: 6g, Fiber: 6g

Homemade Beef Tacos with Avocado

INGREDIENTS

1/2 pound ground beef
1 tablespoon taco seasoning
4 small soft or hard taco shells
1 avocado, sliced
1/4 cup shredded lettuce
1/4 cup diced tomatoes
1/4 cup shredded cheddar
cheese

2 SERVINGS	**10 MINS** PERP TIME	**10 MINS** COOK TIME

INSTRUCTIONS

1. Cook the ground beef until browned in a pan, breaking it apart as it cooks. Drain any excess fat.
2. Add taco seasoning and a few tablespoons of water. Simmer for 2-3 minutes until the seasoning is absorbed.
3. Warm the taco shells in a separate pan or microwave.
4. Fill each taco shell with the seasoned beef, then top with avocado slices, shredded lettuce, diced tomatoes, and cheddar cheese.
5. Serve immediately.

NUTRITIONAL VALUES (PER SERVING):

Calories: 350, Protein: 20g,
Carbohydrates: 28g, Fat: 18g, Fiber: 6g

Teriyaki Chicken and Rice Bowls

2	**10 MINS**	**15 MINS**
SERVINGS	PERP TIME	COOK TIME

INGREDIENTS

1 chicken breast, cut into bite-sized pieces
1/4 cup teriyaki sauce
1/2 cup broccoli florets, steamed
1/2 cup carrots, sliced
1/2 cup cooked rice
1 tablespoon olive oil

INSTRUCTIONS

1. In a large pan, heat one tablespoon of oil over medium heat. Add meat pieces and cook for 5-7 minutes until cooked through.
2. Pour the teriyaki sauce and stir well to coat. Cook more for 2-3 minutes until the sauce thickens.
3. Divide the cooked rice between two bowls.
4. Top the rice with the teriyaki chicken, steamed broccoli, and carrots.
5. Serve immediately.

NUTRITIONAL VALUES (PER SERVING):

Calories: 350, Protein: 28g,
Carbohydrates: 40g, Fat: 8g, Fiber: 4g

Cheesy Spinach and Ricotta Calzones

INGREDIENTS

1/2 cup ricotta cheese
1/4 cup shredded mozzarella cheese
1/2 cup spinach, chopped
1 teaspoon garlic powder
1 refrigerated pizza dough
1 tablespoon olive oil
Marinara sauce (for dipping)

2
SERVINGS

10 MINS
PERP TIME

15 MINS
COOK TIME

INSTRUCTIONS

1. Preheat oven to 375°F (190°C). Arrange the baking sheet with parchment paper.
2. In a deep-bottom bowl, mix the ricotta, mozzarella, spinach, and garlic powder. Roll out the pizza dough and cut it into two equal portions.
3. Spoon the cheese and spinach mixture onto one side of each dough portion, leaving space around the edges.
4. Fold the dough and pinch the edges to seal. Brush the tops with olive oil. Bake for 12-15 minutes, or until golden brown. Serve with marinara sauce for dipping.

NUTRITIONAL VALUES (PER SERVING):

Calories: 320, Protein: 14g,
Carbohydrates: 36g, Fat: 14g, Fiber: 2g

THIRST QUENCHERS

Tropical Paradise Smoothie

INGREDIENTS

1/2 cup pineapple chunks (fresh or frozen)
1/2 cup mango chunks (fresh or frozen)
1/2 cup coconut milk
1/2 cup orange juice
1 tablespoon honey (optional)

2
SERVINGS

5 MINS
PERP TIME

00 MINS
COOK TIME

INSTRUCTIONS

1. Place the pineapple, mango, coconut milk, and orange juice into a blender.
2. Blend the ingredients on full power until the texture turns smooth and creamy.
3. Taste and add honey if additional sweetness is desired.
4. Pour into the wide-mouth glasses or jars and serve immediately.

NUTRITIONAL VALUES (PER SERVING):

Calories: 130, Protein: 1g,
Carbohydrates: 31g, Fat: 3g, Fiber: 2g

Strawberry Banana Swirl Milkshake

INGREDIENTS

1 cup vanilla ice cream
1/2 cup milk
1/2 cup strawberries, hulled
1 banana, sliced
Whipped cream (optional for topping)

2
SERVINGS

5 MINS
PERP TIME

00 MINS
COOK TIME

INSTRUCTIONS

1. In a food blender, blend the vanilla ice cream, milk, and banana until smooth.
2. Drop half of the mixture into two glasses.
3. Add the strawberries to the remaining milkshake mixture in the food blender and blend thoroughly.
4. Pour the strawberry mixture on top of the banana mixture into the glasses to create a swirl effect.
5. Top with whipped cream and serve immediately.

NUTRITIONAL VALUES (PER SERVING):

Calories: 220, Protein: 4g,
Carbohydrates: 38g, Fat: 7g, Fiber: 3g

CLASSIC FRESH LEMONADE

INGREDIENTS

1/2 cup lemon juice
2 cups cold water
2 tablespoons honey or sugar
(to taste)
Ice cubes
Lemon slices for garnish
(optional)

2
SERVINGS

5 MINS
PERP TIME

00 MINS
COOK TIME

INSTRUCTIONS

1. In a pitcher, combine the lemon juice, cold water, and honey or sugar.
2. Stir well until the honey or sugar is fully dissolved.
3. Fill two glasses with ice and ladle lemonade over the ice.
4. Put lemon slice on top if desired, and serve immediately.

NUTRITIONAL VALUES (PER SERVING):

Calories: 60, Protein: 0g, Carbohydrates:
17g, Fat: 0g, Fiber: 0g

BERRY BLAST SMOOTHIE

2
SERVINGS

5 MINS
PERP TIME

00 MINS
COOK TIME

INGREDIENTS

1/2 cup strawberries (fresh or frozen)

1/2 cup blueberries (fresh or frozen)

1/2 cup raspberries (fresh or frozen)

1/2 cup Greek yogurt

1/2 cup almond milk

1 tablespoon honey (optional)

INSTRUCTIONS

1. Place the strawberries, blueberries, raspberries, Greek yogurt, and milk into a blender.
2. Blend the ingredients on full power until the texture turns smooth and creamy.
3. Taste and add more sweetener (honey) if desired for extra sweetness.
4. Pour into the wide-mouth glasses or jars and serve immediately.

NUTRITIONAL VALUES (PER SERVING):

Calories: 150, Protein: 6g,
Carbohydrates: 30g, Fat: 2g, Fiber: 6g

Watermelon Cooler Slushie

2
SERVINGS

5 MINS
PERP TIME

00 MINS
COOK TIME

INGREDIENTS

2 cups watermelon chunks,
seedless
1/2 cup ice cubes
1 tablespoon lime juice
1 tablespoon honey (optional)
Mint leaves for garnish
(optional)

INSTRUCTIONS

1. Place the watermelon chunks, ice cubes, lime juice, and honey into a blender.
2. Blend until smooth and slushy.
3. Pour into the wide-mouth glasses or jars and garnish with mint leaves if desired. Serve immediately.

NUTRITIONAL VALUES (PER SERVING):

Calories: 80, Protein: 1g, Carbohydrates:
21g, Fat: 0g, Fiber: 1g

Mango Pineapple Smoothie

INGREDIENTS

1/2 cup mango chunks (fresh or frozen)
1/2 cup pineapple chunks (fresh or frozen)
1/2 cup regular water
1/2 cup Greek yogurt
1 tablespoon honey (optional)

2
SERVINGS

5 MINS
PERP TIME

00 MINS
COOK TIME

INSTRUCTIONS

1. Place the mango, pineapple, water, and Greek yogurt into a blender.
2. Blend the ingredients on full power until the texture turns smooth and creamy.
3. Taste and add honey if additional sweetness is desired.
4. Pour into the wide-mouth glasses or jars and serve immediately.

NUTRITIONAL VALUES (PER SERVING):

Calories: 130, Protein: 5g,
Carbohydrates: 26g, Fat: 2g, Fiber: 3g

Minty Cucumber Lime Water

2
SERVINGS

5 MINS
PERP TIME

00 MINS
COOK TIME

INGREDIENTS

1/2 cucumber, thinly sliced
1 lime, thinly sliced
4-5 fresh mint leaves
2 cups cold water
Ice cubes

INSTRUCTIONS

1. In a pitcher, combine the cucumber slices, lime slices, and mint leaves.
2. Add the cold water and stir gently.
3. Fill two glasses with ice cubes. Ladle the infused water over the ice.
4. Serve immediately, or let it sit for a few minutes to allow the flavors to blend.

NUTRITIONAL VALUES (PER SERVING):

Calories: 10, Protein: 0g, Carbohydrates: 3g, Fat: 0g, Fiber: 1g

Blueberry Vanilla Smoothie

INGREDIENTS

1/2 cup blueberries (fresh or frozen)
1/2 cup vanilla Greek yogurt
1/2 cup almond milk
1 teaspoon vanilla extract
1 tablespoon honey (optional)

2
SERVINGS

5 MINS
PERP TIME

00 MINS
COOK TIME

INSTRUCTIONS

1. Place the blueberries, vanilla yogurt, milk, and vanilla extract into a blender.
2. Blend the ingredients on full power until the texture turns smooth and creamy.
3. Taste and add more sweetener (honey) if desired for extra sweetness.
4. Pour into the wide-mouth glasses or jars and serve immediately.

NUTRITIONAL VALUES (PER SERVING):

Calories: 140, Protein: 6g,
Carbohydrates: 26g, Fat: 2g, Fiber: 3g

Raspberry Lemonade Spritzer

INGREDIENTS

1/2 cup raspberries (fresh or frozen)
1/2 cup freshly squeezed lemon juice
1 tablespoon honey (optional)
1 cup sparkling water
Ice cubes

2
SERVINGS

5 MINS
PERP TIME

00 MINS
COOK TIME

INSTRUCTIONS

1. In a food blender, blend the raspberries, lemon juice, and honey until smooth.
2. Strain the mixture if desired to remove the raspberry seeds.
3. Fill the glasses with ice. Divide the raspberry lemonade mixture between them.
4. Top with sparkling water, stir gently and serve immediately.

NUTRITIONAL VALUES (PER SERVING):

Calories: 60, Protein: 1g, Carbohydrates: 17g, Fat: 0g, Fiber: 4g

Orange Creamsicle Shake

INGREDIENTS

1/2 cup orange juice
1/2 cup vanilla ice cream
1/2 cup Greek yogurt
1 teaspoon vanilla extract
1 tablespoon honey (optional)

2
SERVINGS

5 MINS
PERP TIME

00 MINS
COOK TIME

INSTRUCTIONS

1. Place the orange juice, vanilla ice cream, Greek yogurt, and vanilla extract into a blender.
2. Blend the ingredients on full power until the texture turns smooth and creamy.
3. Taste and add more sweetener (honey) if desired for extra sweetness.
4. Pour into the wide-mouth glasses or jars and serve immediately.

NUTRITIONAL VALUES (PER SERVING):

Calories: 180, Protein: 6g,
Carbohydrates: 32g, Fat: 4g, Fiber: 0g

Peach Iced Tea with Fresh Mint

INGREDIENTS

2 black tea bags
2 ripe peaches, sliced
4 cups water
1 tablespoon honey (optional)
Fresh mint leaves for garnish
Ice cubes

2
SERVINGS

5 MINS
PERP TIME

5 MINS
COOK TIME

INSTRUCTIONS

1. Add 4 cups water to a boil, add tea bags and keep them to steep for 5 minutes. Remove the tea bags and put it aside to cool.
2. In a pitcher, combine the sliced peaches, honey (if using), and cooled tea. Stir gently.
3. Refrigerate for one hour (at least) to allow the flavors to blend.
4. Serve the peach iced tea over ice cubes and garnish with fresh mint leaves.

NUTRITIONAL VALUES (PER SERVING):

Calories: 60, Protein: 0g, Carbohydrates: 16g, Fat: 0g, Fiber: 1g

MIXED BERRY INFUSED WATER

INGREDIENTS

1/4 cup strawberries, halved
1/4 cup blueberries
1/4 cup raspberries
4 cups cold water
Ice cubes

2
SERVINGS

5 MINS
PERP TIME

00 MINS
COOK TIME

INSTRUCTIONS

1. In a pitcher, combine the strawberries, blueberries, and raspberries.
2. Pour the cold water over the berries and stir gently.
3. Let the mixture sit for 5-10 minutes to allow the flavors to infuse.
4. Fill two wide-mouth glasses with ice cubes, pour the berry-infused water, and serve immediately.

NUTRITIONAL VALUES (PER SERVING):

Calories: 10, Protein: 0g, Carbohydrates: 2g, Fat: 0g, Fiber: 1g

Banana Nutella Milkshake

INGREDIENTS

1 ripe banana, sliced
1/4 cup Nutella
1 cup milk (any type)
1/2 cup vanilla ice cream
Whipped cream (optional for topping)

2
SERVINGS

5 MINS
PERP TIME

00 MINS
COOK TIME

INSTRUCTIONS

1. In a food blender, combine the sliced banana, Nutella, milk, and vanilla ice cream.
2. Blend the ingredients on full power until the texture turns smooth and creamy.
3. Pour into the wide-mouth glasses or jars top with whipped cream if desired. Serve immediately.

NUTRITIONAL VALUES (PER SERVING):

Calories: 310, Protein: 6g,
Carbohydrates: 42g, Fat: 14g, Fiber: 2g

Pineapple Coconut Smoothie

INGREDIENTS

1/2 cup pineapple chunks
(fresh or frozen)
1/2 cup coconut milk
1/2 cup Greek yogurt
1 tablespoon honey (optional)

2
SERVINGS

5 MINS
PERP TIME

00 MINS
COOK TIME

INSTRUCTIONS

1. Place the pineapple chunks, coconut milk, and Greek yogurt into a blender.
2. Blend the ingredients on full power until the texture turns smooth and creamy.
3. Taste and add honey if additional sweetness is desired.
4. Pour into the wide-mouth glasses or jars and serve immediately.

NUTRITIONAL VALUES (PER SERVING):

Calories: 160, Protein: 5g,
Carbohydrates: 24g, Fat: 6g, Fiber: 2g

111

Cherry Limeade Slushie

INGREDIENTS

1 cup cherries (fresh or frozen), pitted
1/4 cup freshly squeezed lime juice
1 tablespoon honey
1/2 cup ice cubes
Lime wedges for garnish (optional)

2
SERVINGS

5 MINS
PERP TIME

00 MINS
COOK TIME

INSTRUCTIONS

1. Place the cherries, lime juice, honey, and ice cubes into a blender.
2. Blend until smooth and slushy.
3. Pour into the wide-mouth glasses or jars and garnish with lime wedges if desired. Serve immediately.

NUTRITIONAL VALUES (PER SERVING):

Calories: 110, Protein: 1g,
Carbohydrates: 28g, Fat: 0g, Fiber: 3g

Caramel Apple Smoothie

2
SERVINGS

5 MINS
PERP TIME

00 MINS
COOK TIME

INGREDIENTS

1 apple, peeled, cored, and sliced
1/2 cup Greek yogurt
1/2 cup milk (any type)
2 tablespoons caramel sauce
1/2 teaspoon cinnamon
Ice cubes

INSTRUCTIONS

1. Place the apple slices, Greek yogurt, milk, caramel sauce, cinnamon, and ice cubes into a blender.
2. Blend the ingredients on full power until the texture turns smooth and creamy.
3. Pour into the wide-mouth glasses or jars and drizzle with extra caramel sauce if desired. Serve immediately.

NUTRITIONAL VALUES (PER SERVING):

Calories: 180, Protein: 5g,
Carbohydrates: 32g, Fat: 4g, Fiber: 3g

Tropical Mango Lassi

INGREDIENTS

1 cup mango chunks (fresh or frozen)
1/2 cup plain Greek yogurt
1/2 cup water or milk
1 tablespoon honey (optional)
A pinch of cardamom (optional)

2
SERVINGS

5 MINS
PERP TIME

00 MINS
COOK TIME

INSTRUCTIONS

1. Place the mango, Greek yogurt, water or milk, honey, and cardamom into a blender.
2. Blend the ingredients on full power until the texture turns smooth and creamy.
3. Pour into the wide-mouth glasses or jars and serve immediately.

NUTRITIONAL VALUES (PER SERVING):

Calories: 140, Protein: 6g,
Carbohydrates: 28g, Fat: 1g, Fiber: 3g

Vanilla Almond Milkshake

INGREDIENTS

1 cup almond milk
1/2 cup vanilla ice cream
1/2 teaspoon vanilla extract
1 tablespoon almond butter
Ice cubes

2
SERVINGS

5 MINS
PERP TIME

00 MINS
COOK TIME

INSTRUCTIONS

1. Place the almond milk, vanilla ice cream, vanilla extract, almond butter, and ice cubes into a blender.
2. Blend the ingredients on full power until the texture turns smooth and creamy.
3. Pour into the wide-mouth glasses or jars and serve immediately.

NUTRITIONAL VALUES (PER SERVING):

Calories: 200, Protein: 4g,
Carbohydrates: 25g, Fat: 10g, Fiber: 1g

Chocolate Chip Cookie Milkshake

INGREDIENTS

1 cup milk (any type)
1/2 cup vanilla ice cream
2 chocolate chip cookies crumbled
1 tablespoon chocolate chips
Whipped cream (optional for topping)

2
SERVINGS

5 MINS
PERP TIME

00 MINS
COOK TIME

INSTRUCTIONS

1. In a food blender, combine the milk, vanilla ice cream, crumbled chocolate chip cookies, and chocolate chips.
2. Blend the ingredients on full power until the texture turns smooth and creamy.
3. Pour into the wide-mouth glasses or jars top with whipped cream if desired. Serve immediately.

NUTRITIONAL VALUES (PER SERVING):

Calories: 320, Protein: 6g,
Carbohydrates: 44g, Fat: 14g, Fiber: 1g

RASPBERRY PEACH LEMONADE

INGREDIENTS

1/2 cup raspberries (fresh or frozen)
1 peach, pitted and sliced
1/2 cup freshly squeezed lemon juice
1 tablespoon honey (optional)
1 cup cold water
Ice cubes

2
SERVINGS

5 MINS
PERP TIME

00 MINS
COOK TIME

INSTRUCTIONS

1. In a food blender, blend the raspberries, peach slices, lemon juice, honey, and cold water until smooth.
2. Strain the mixture if desired to remove seeds.
3. Fill two wide-mouth glasses with ice cubes and pour the lemonade over the ice. Serve immediately.

NUTRITIONAL VALUES (PER SERVING):

Calories: 80, Protein: 1g, Carbohydrates: 20g, Fat: 0g, Fiber: 3g

Sweet Treats

Frozen Yogurt Fruit Pops

INGREDIENTS

1 cup plain Greek yogurt
1 tablespoon honey
1/2 cup mixed berries
1/2 cup diced mango
Popsicle molds or small paper
cups with sticks

4
SERVINGS

10 MINS
PERP TIME

00 MINS
COOK TIME

INSTRUCTIONS

1. In a deep-bottom bowl, mix the Greek yogurt and honey until well combined.
2. Divide the mixed berries and diced mango among the popsicle molds or cups.
3. Spoon the honey yogurt mixture over the fruit, filling the molds.
4. Insert the sticks and freeze them for at least 4 hours or until fully frozen.
5. Once frozen, remove the yogurt pops from the molds and enjoy!

NUTRITIONAL VALUES (PER SERVING):

Calories: 80, Protein: 5g, Carbohydrates:
15g, Fat: 1g, Fiber: 2g

No-Bake Strawberry Cheesecake Cups

2
SERVINGS

10 MINS
PERP TIME

00 MINS
COOK TIME

INGREDIENTS

1/2 cup graham cracker crumbs
2 tablespoons melted butter
1/2 cup cream cheese, softened
1/4 cup Greek yogurt
2 tablespoons honey
1/2 cup sliced strawberries

INSTRUCTIONS

1. In a small, deep-bottom bowl, mix the graham cracker crumbs and melted butter. Divide the mixture equall into two serving cups and press down to form a crust.
2. In another deep-bottom bowl, mix the softened cream cheese, Greek yogurt, and honey until smooth.
3. Spoon cream cheese mixture on graham cracker crusts top.
4. Top with sliced strawberries and refrigerate for at least 1 hour before serving.

NUTRITIONAL VALUES (PER SERVING):

Calories: 220, Protein: 5g,
Carbohydrates: 28g, Fat: 10g, Fiber: 1g

Chocolate-Dipped Banana Bites

INGREDIENTS

2 bananas, sliced
1/2 cup dark chocolate chips
1 tablespoon coconut oil
1 tablespoon chopped nuts
(optional)

2
SERVINGS

5 MINS
PERP TIME

00 MINS
COOK TIME

INSTRUCTIONS

1. Place the banana slices on a parchment paper-arranged baking sheet and freeze for 30 minutes.
2. In a microwave-safe or glass bowl, melt the chocolate chips with coconut oil together, stirring until smooth.
3. Dip each frozen banana slice halfway into the melted oil chocolate mixture, then place them back on the baking sheet.
4. Sprinkle with chopped nuts if desired and freeze for another 15 minutes until the chocolate is set.
5. Serve frozen, and enjoy!

NUTRITIONAL VALUES (PER SERVING):

Calories: 180, Protein: 2g,
Carbohydrates: 32g, Fat: 7g, Fiber: 3g

Mini Fruit Tarts with Whipped Cream

INGREDIENTS

4 mini graham cracker tart shells
1/2 cup whipped cream
1/2 cup mixed fruit (strawberries, blueberries, kiwi)
1 tablespoon honey (optional)

4
SERVINGS

10 MINS
PERP TIME

00 MINS
COOK TIME

INSTRUCTIONS

1. Fill each mini tart shell with a spoonful of whipped cream.
2. Arrange the mixed fruit on top of the whipped cream in each tart.
3. Drizzle honey on top if desired and serve immediately.

NUTRITIONAL VALUES (PER SERVING):

Calories: 150, Protein: 2g,
Carbohydrates: 24g, Fat: 6g, Fiber: 2g

No-Bake Oreo Cheesecake Bars

INGREDIENTS

1 cup Oreo cookie crumbs
(about 12 Oreos)
3 tablespoons melted butter
1/2 cup cream cheese,
softened
1/4 cup powdered sugar
1/2 teaspoon vanilla extract
1/4 cup whipped cream

4	**15 MINS**	**00 MINS**
SERVINGS	PERP TIME	COOK TIME

INSTRUCTIONS

1. In a small, deep-bottom bowl, mix the Oreo cookie crumbs and melted butter. Press the mixture toward the bottom of a greased or parchment paper-arranged small baking dish to form a crust.
2. In another deep-bottom bowl, mix the cream cheese, powdered sugar, and vanilla extract until smooth.
3. Toss in the whipped cream until fully incorporated.
4. Spread cream cheese mixture over the crust and refrigerate for at least 2 hours to set.
5. Slice into bars and serve chilled.

NUTRITIONAL VALUES (PER SERVING):

Calories: 260, Protein: 3g,
Carbohydrates: 30g, Fat: 14g, Fiber: 1g

Rainbow Jello Parfaits

INGREDIENTS

1 box (3 oz) strawberry Jello
1 box (3 oz) lemon Jello
1 box (3 oz) lime Jello
1 1/2 cups whipped cream (for layering)

4
SERVINGS

15 MINS
PERP TIME

00 MINS
COOK TIME

INSTRUCTIONS

1. Prepare the strawberry Jello according to the steps mentioned on the package instructions and let it cool slightly. Pour into 4 serving cups, filling each about 1/3 full. Refrigerate until set (about 1 hour).
2. Once the strawberry layer is set, add a spoonful of whipped cream over each layer.
3. Prepare the lemon Jello, let it cool slightly, and pour it over the whipped cream layer. Refrigerate until set.
4. Repeat the process with the lime Jello and finish with a final whipped cream dollop on top. Serve chilled.

NUTRITIONAL VALUES (PER SERVING):

Calories: 120, Protein: 2g,
Carbohydrates: 25g, Fat: 3g, Fiber: 0g

No-Bake Peanut Butter Chocolate Fudge

INGREDIENTS

1/2 cup peanut butter
1/2 cup dark chocolate chips
2 tablespoons coconut oil
1/4 cup powdered sugar
1/2 teaspoon vanilla extract

8
SERVINGS

10 MINS
PERP TIME

00 MINS
COOK TIME

INSTRUCTIONS

1. In a microwave-safe bowl, melt the peanut butter, chocolate chips, and coconut oil stirring in between time intervals until smooth.
2. Toss in the powdered sugar and vanilla extract until well combined.
3. Drop the mixture into a small baking dish arranged on parchment paper and smooth it on top.
4. Refrigerate for at least 2 hours or until firm. Cut into small squares and serve chilled.

NUTRITIONAL VALUES (PER SERVING):

Calories: 160, Protein: 3g,
Carbohydrates: 14g, Fat: 10g, Fiber: 1g

Strawberry Shortcake Skewers

INGREDIENTS

1 cup cubed angel food cake
1 cup fresh strawberries, halved
1/2 cup whipped cream
Wooden or reusable skewers

4
SERVINGS

10 MINS
PERP TIME

00 MINS
COOK TIME

INSTRUCTIONS

1. Thread the angel food cake cubes and strawberry halves alternately onto the skewers.
2. Arrange skewers on the shallow serving plate and drizzle with whipped cream on the side for dipping.
3. Serve immediately as a fun and light dessert.

NUTRITIONAL VALUES (PER SERVING):

Calories: 120, Protein: 2g,
Carbohydrates: 25g, Fat: 3g, Fiber: 2g

Chocolate-Covered Strawberry Pops

INGREDIENTS

12 large strawberries
1/2 cup dark chocolate chips
1 tablespoon coconut oil
4 wooden sticks

4	**10 MINS**	**00 MINS**
SERVINGS	PERP TIME	COOK TIME

INSTRUCTIONS

1. Insert a wooden stick into the top of each strawberry.
2. In a microwave-safe or glass bowl, melt the chocolate chips with coconut oil stirring in between until smooth.
3. Dip each strawberry into the melted oil chocolate mixture, covering about 3/4 of the strawberry.
4. Place the dipped strawberries on a parchment paper-arranged baking sheet and refrigerate for 10-15 minutes until the chocolate is set.
5. Serve chilled as a refreshing and fun treat.

NUTRITIONAL VALUES (PER SERVING):

Calories: 120, Protein: 1g,
Carbohydrates: 15g, Fat: 7g, Fiber: 3g

127

No-Bake Lemon Icebox Bars

INGREDIENTS

1 1/2 cups graham cracker crumbs
1/4 cup melted butter
1 cup cream cheese, softened
1/4 cup lemon juice
1/4 cup sweetened condensed milk
1 teaspoon lemon zest

8
SERVINGS

10 MINS
PERP TIME

00 MINS
COOK TIME

INSTRUCTIONS

1. In a small, deep-bottom bowl, mix the graham cracker crumbs and melted butter. Press the mixture toward the bottom of a greased or parchment paper-arranged small baking dish to form a crust.
2. In another deep-bottom bowl, mix the cream cheese, lemon juice, condensed milk (sweetened), and lemon zest until smooth.
3. Spread the lemon mixture evenly over the graham cracker crust.
4. Refrigerate for at least 2 hours or until firm. Slice into bars and serve chilled.

NUTRITIONAL VALUES (PER SERVING):

Calories: 220, Protein: 3g,
Carbohydrates: 25g, Fat: 12g, Fiber: 0g

Banana Split Sundae Boats

2	5 MINS	00 MINS
SERVINGS	PERP TIME	COOK TIME

INGREDIENTS

2 bananas, peeled and half lengthwise

1/2 cup vanilla ice cream

1/4 cup chocolate syrup

1/4 cup whipped cream

2 tablespoons chopped nuts (optional)

4 maraschino cherries

INSTRUCTIONS

1. Place the banana halves in two shallow bowls or plates.
2. Scoop the ice cream into the center of each banana "boat."
3. Drizzle chocolate syrup over ice cream and bananas.
4. Top with whipped cream, chopped nuts, and maraschino cherries. Serve immediately.

NUTRITIONAL VALUES (PER SERVING):

Calories: 290, Protein: 4g,
Carbohydrates: 50g, Fat: 12g, Fiber: 3g

S'mores Dip with Graham Crackers

INGREDIENTS

1/2 cup milk chocolate chips
1/2 cup mini marshmallows
4 graham crackers, broken into pieces

2
SERVINGS

5 MINS
PERP TIME

5 MINS
COOK TIME

INSTRUCTIONS

1. Preheat oven to 375°F (190°C).
2. In a small oven-safe dish, layer the chocolate chips and mini marshmallows.
3. Bake for 3-5 minutes until the chocolate is melt thoroughly and the marshmallows are golden brown.
4. Remove and serve immediately.

NUTRITIONAL VALUES (PER SERVING):

Calories: 250, Protein: 3g,
Carbohydrates: 40g, Fat: 10g, Fiber: 2g

No-Bake Mini Cheesecake Bites

INGREDIENTS

1/2 cup graham cracker crumbs
2 tablespoons melted butter
1/2 cup cream cheese, softened
2 tablespoons powdered sugar
1/4 teaspoon vanilla extract
Fresh berries for topping

4
SERVINGS

15 MINS
PERP TIME

00 MINS
COOK TIME

INSTRUCTIONS

1. In a small, deep-bottom bowl, mix the graham cracker crumbs and melted butter. Press the mixture toward the bottom of mini muffin cups to form a crust.
2. In another deep-bottom bowl, mix the cream cheese, powdered sugar, and vanilla extract until smooth.
3. Drop cream cheese mixture over the graham cracker crusts and smooth the tops.
4. Refrigerate for at least 2 hours until set.
5. Top with fresh berries before serving.

NUTRITIONAL VALUES (PER SERVING):

Calories: 180, Protein: 3g,
Carbohydrates: 16g, Fat: 12g, Fiber: 1g

Frozen Banana Yogurt Bites

INGREDIENTS

1 banana, sliced
1/2 cup Greek yogurt
1 tablespoon honey
1 tablespoon mini chocolate
chips (optional)

2
SERVINGS

10 MINS
PERP TIME

00 MINS
COOK TIME

INSTRUCTIONS

1. Dip each banana slice into the Greek yogurt, ensuring it's fully coated.
2. Place the coated banana slices on a parchment paper-arranged baking sheet.
3. Drizzle honey over the banana slices and sprinkle with mini chocolate chips if desired.
4. Freeze for 1-2 hours or until the yogurt is firm. Serve frozen.

NUTRITIONAL VALUES (PER SERVING):

Calories: 130, Protein: 5g,
Carbohydrates: 28g, Fat: 2g, Fiber: 2g

No-Bake Vanilla Cake Pops

| **4** | **10 MINS** | **00 MINS** |
| SERVINGS | PERP TIME | COOK TIME |

INGREDIENTS

1 cup vanilla cake crumbs
(use store-bought cake or
homemade)
1/4 cup cream cheese frosting
1/2 cup white chocolate chips
Sprinkles for decoration
8 lollipop sticks

INSTRUCTIONS

1. In a deep-bottom bowl, mix the vanilla cake crumbs and cream cheese frosting until fully combined.
2. Roll the mixture into 1-inch balls and insert a lollipop stick into each ball.
3. Place the cake pops on a parchment paper-arranged baking sheet and freeze for 15-20 minutes.
4. Melt the white chocolate chips using the microwave-safe or glass bowl, stirring until smooth.
5. Dip each cake piece into the melted white chocolate and decorate with sprinkles. Let them set before serving.

NUTRITIONAL VALUES (PER SERVING):

Calories: 200, Protein: 2g,
Carbohydrates: 25g, Fat: 10g, Fiber: 0g

Caramel Apple Nachos

INGREDIENTS

2 medium apples, cored and thinly sliced

2 tablespoons caramel sauce

2 tablespoons chopped peanuts or almonds

2 tablespoons mini chocolate chips

2
SERVINGS

5 MINS
PERP TIME

00 MINS
COOK TIME

INSTRUCTIONS

1. Arrange the apple slices on the shallow serving plate.
2. Drizzle caramel sauce evenly over the aarranged slices.
3. Sprinkle the chopped peanuts and mini chocolate chips on top.
4. Serve immediately as a fun, healthy snack.

NUTRITIONAL VALUES (PER SERVING):

Calories: 220, Protein: 2g,
Carbohydrates: 48g, Fat: 6g, Fiber: 5g

No-Bake Coconut Macaroons

INGREDIENTS

1 1/2 cups shredded coconut

1/4 cup sweetened condensed milk

1/2 teaspoon vanilla extract

1/4 cup melted dark chocolate (optional)

2
SERVINGS

10 MINS
PERP TIME

00 MINS
COOK TIME

INSTRUCTIONS

1. In a deep-bottom bowl, mix the shredded coconut, sweetened condensed milk, and vanilla extract.
2. Scoop tablespoon-sized portions of the mixture and form them into small mounds. Place them on a parchment paper-arranged baking sheet.
3. Refrigerate for at least 1 hour to set.
4. Optional: Drizzle with melted dark chocolate before serving.

NUTRITIONAL VALUES (PER SERVING):

Calories: 170, Protein: 2g,
Carbohydrates: 18g, Fat: 10g, Fiber: 2g

No-Bake Peanut Butter Oat Bars

INGREDIENTS

1 1/2 cups rolled oats
1/2 cup peanut butter
1/4 cup honey
1/4 cup mini chocolate chips
(optional)

4
SERVINGS

10 MINS
PERP TIME

00 MINS
COOK TIME

INSTRUCTIONS

1. In a microwave-safe bowl, heat the peanut butter and honey together for 30 seconds. Stir until smooth.
2. In a deep-bottom bowl, mix the rolled oats with the peanut butter and honey mixture until fully combined.
3. Press the mixture softly toward the greased or parchment paper-arranged small baking dish.
4. Spread the mini chocolate chips on top and press them into the mixture.
5. Refrigerate for at least 1 hour to set, then cut into bars.

NUTRITIONAL VALUES (PER SERVING):

Calories: 250, Protein: 6g,
Carbohydrates: 30g, Fat: 12g, Fiber: 4g

Chocolate Rice Cereal Treats

4
SERVINGS

10 MINS
PERP TIME

00 MINS
COOK TIME

INGREDIENTS

3 cups crispy rice cereal
1/2 cup dark chocolate chips
1/4 cup peanut butter
2 tablespoons honey

INSTRUCTIONS

1. In a microwave-safe or glass bowl, melt the chocolate chips, peanut butter, and honey together in 30-second intervals, stirring until smooth.
2. In a deep-bottom bowl, mix the crispy rice cereal with the melted chocolate mixture until the cereal is fully coated.
3. Press the mixture softly toward a greased or parchment paper-arranged small baking dish.
4. Refrigerate for at least 1 hour to set, then cut into squares.

NUTRITIONAL VALUES (PER SERVING):

Calories: 200, Protein: 4g,
Carbohydrates: 28g, Fat: 8g, Fiber: 2g

CONCLUSION

Congratulations, young chef! You've journeyed through the kitchen, learned new skills, and created delicious dishes along the way. From the first time you picked up a spoon to your latest masterpiece, you've discovered that cooking is not just about making food—it's about creativity, patience, and having fun.

As you've explored the pages of The Essential Young Chefs Cookbook, you've gained confidence in the kitchen, learned the importance of safety, and discovered the joy of sharing meals with family and friends. Remember, every great chef started just like you—with curiosity, a love for food, and a willingness to learn.

Cooking is a lifelong adventure, and now that you have the basics down, there are endless possibilities ahead. Whether you're making breakfast for the family, whipping up a quick snack, or experimenting with new flavors, know that the kitchen is your canvas. Don't be afraid to make mistakes—they're just stepping stones on the path to becoming an even better cook.

Keep this cookbook close as you continue to explore and create. Try new recipes, tweak the ones you love, and most importantly, enjoy the process. Cooking is about expressing yourself and bringing joy to others through food, one dish at a time.

Thank you for letting this cookbook be a part of your culinary journey. Now, it's time to take what you've learned and continue creating delicious memories in the kitchen. Remember, every dish you make is a celebration of your skills, imagination, and love for food.

Happy cooking, and may your kitchen adventures always be filled with flavor, fun, and a sprinkle of magic!